THE ANTI-SEMITE

Pascal Boniface

The Anti-Semite

Max Milo Éditions, Paris, 2023
www.maxmilo.com
ISBN : 978-2-315-02135-2

In memory of Stéphane Hessel
To André Schmer

Foreword by Michel Wieviorka

When Pascal Boniface asked me to write this preface, I thought it was no small invitation. Introducing the work of someone accused of anti-Semitism is no mean feat!

Here we have a researcher, Pascal Boniface, whose political and geopolitical analyses are said to be biased and oriented—a commonplace occurrence in such matters!—and also motivated by hatred of Jews and the State of Israel: a heavy accusation. Here we have the founder and director of a research institute, IRIS, whose existence is threatened and whose operations weakened on the basis of the same accusations: this is a serious matter, since it affects not only a person, but also an institution dedicated to the production and dissemination of knowledge.

What is the basis for the suspicion that turns into denunciation? Unless you consider that any criticism of Israeli policy is necessarily tainted by anti-Semitism, the accusations hardly hold water. You can disagree politically with Pascal Boniface, of course, and not share his friendships or enmities: that in no way justifies the torrents of mud that have been poured on him for over fifteen years, with a bias that I have witnessed first-hand on several occasions.

Yes, the debate in France constantly gets out of hand when it comes to Islam, Muslims and Jews. Yes, particularly threatening verbal violence can be used in France against anyone who dares to criticize the policies of the Hebrew state. Yes, committed Jewish intellectuals, activists and institutional leaders prefer the disqualification of political opponents to reasoned debate, invective and indictment to any effort to listen to or read honestly those who do not think as they do, and who are not, for all that, horrible racists.

And what a disqualification, what an accusation! After all, no one can ignore the fact that anti-Semitism is a crime, and not simply a matter of opinion. And that anyone who professes it is therefore a criminal. Necessarily criminal. The diagnosis generally leaves the accused without a reply, without the ability to defend himself or make his voice heard, so serious and shocking is the crime. More often than not, the media condemn, and public opinion follows, without any serene, documented judgment: which is exactly what happened to Pascal Boniface.

As it happens, I too have sometimes had to suffer, albeit on a small scale, from behavior and remarks of the type described by Pascal Boniface. But with the exception that it's hard to suspect someone like me of anti-Semitism—although a Jewish intellectual can sometimes be taken to court on this charge, as Edgar Morin knows all about it—and that an argument is sometimes brandished, without demonstration, to explain supposed anti-Semitism on the part of Jews: that they are driven by self-hatred.

It's painful to be hated and rejected by people and groups who distort your writings, confuse sociological analysis with ideological position-taking, stigmatize, exert pressure to ban you from expression, and present themselves as the guarantors of values that they in fact misappropriate or pervert. In the past, I have known and appreciated the CRIF of Théo Klein or Henri Hajdenberg, a humanist organization, open to intellectual life, to the debate of ideas, enamored of justice and social progress. I have also seen how Roger Cukierman's CRIF could turn out to be the opposite, including with me, smearing me shamelessly—from this point of view, there is nothing that surprises me in Boniface's account.

First and foremost, we must hope that this book will put an end once and for all to hateful polemics and stigmatization, which should give way to well-argued exchanges on substance, to which, as I can also testify, Pascal Boniface has never shied away.

But this book should also be read as highlighting two complementary and disturbing phenomena.

In our country, many intellectuals and politicians are quick to denounce communitarianism and defend hyper-republican postures, only to accept that only individuals can be seen in the public space, without being in any way disturbed by the existence of a Jewish communitarianism. French Jews became visible and active as such in the public arena, culturally, politically, against anti-Semitism and in

Foreword by Michel Wieviorka

their relationship with Israel, from the late 1960s onwards. But this mutation calls for little reflection, and even less discussion, in the eyes of some of their most republican organic intellectuals, who do not shy away from criticizing the tendency of other groups, real or otherwise, to operate in a communitarian mode. These people are anti-communitarian... except for their own group!

And, secondly, this Jewish communitarianism quickly becomes indissociable from unconditional support for the policies of the Israeli government, whatever they may be. The same intellectuals and political leaders, in order to be consistent with themselves, quickly become unable to distinguish between criticism of government action in Israel, and virulent anti-Zionism, hostile to the very existence of this state, and quite broadly anti-Semitic. They even seem unaware that in Israel, positions sometimes even more radical than Pascal Boniface's, and at least as critical of government policy as his own, are part of democratic life.

For almost half a century, there has been a lively debate, in France as in other countries, about cultural and then religious differences. Some have argued for their recognition in the public arena, at the risk of encouraging communitarianism; others have preferred to refer to republican principles that push differences into the private sphere, sometimes verging on intolerance. I belong to the small number of people who wonder how to reconcile the universal and the particular, the republican ideal and the recognition of differences, rather than opposing them. It seems to me that those who are most active in their vindictiveness and hatred of Pascal

Boniface belong to an entirely different category: they put forward the Republic as a general principle and at the same time embody Jewish particularism in public life. Perhaps even their verbal violence and excesses are the expression of a kind of ideological schizophrenia.

Pascal Boniface, over and above the criticism that his own analyses and positions deserve, is the man who, in a way, underlines the untenable nature of positions that juxtapose, with no reconciliation other than mythical, republican universalism and adherence to a communitarianism that includes, almost automatically, unconditional support for a foreign state. Debate is not possible for those whose intellectual and moral integrity is jeopardized, and for them, it gives way to violence, verbal at first, but also fraught with physical threats—Boniface knows all about this.

These are important and delicate issues. Pascal Boniface, for the most part, has also avoided slipping into radicalism; he has always been willing to discuss and defend his positions and analyses, and to argue them. I write this preface to do him justice, but also to plead for a society where public debate is less hateful and unfair, where critical thinking can be exercised. Where excess, invective and more or less conspiratorial denunciation give way to argumentation and respect for people. Where we can deal with communitarianism in all its expressions, and not just those we wish to serve or, on the contrary, fight. And where we wage the necessary battle against anti-Semitism where it is rife, without confusing it with a demand for unconditional support for Israeli policy.

Foreword by Michel Wieviorka

Foreword

An intellectual accused of anti-Semitism without ever having uttered or written a sentence that could justify this heavy and infamous incrimination. A research center whose work is recognized nationally and internationally, employing more than thirty people, is in danger of disappearing because its director has criticized the government.

If such a case arose, there's no doubt that in Paris, the media would be outraged and report it widely, while traditional petitioners would mobilize to show their support as loudly as possible. But there was no reaction.

The government criticized was that of a foreign country. And not just any foreign country. Do you think you're in Kafka? No. Welcome to France.

It's Fantastic, Isn't It?

The anti-Semite. That's how I'm perceived by many people, Jews and non-Jews alike. This dishonorable label horrifies me, as I have fought all forms of racism—including anti-Semitism—my entire life. I have been accused of what I consider to be utterly detestable. What's more, it clouds the relationship I can have with many of my fellow Jews, who judge me without knowing me. It constitutes a barrier to the potentially numerous and fruitful relationships I could have established with many of them by arousing fear and/or repulsion.

Beyond private relationships, being considered anti-Semitic is certainly the most powerful reason for exclusion from the public sphere in France. You never come out of such a denunciation unscathed. With this label, you're no match for Lieutenant John McClane, forced to walk through a black neighborhood with a sign reading: "I hate niggers[1]."

Because of its extremely harmful consequences, such a heavy incrimination would have to be strongly substantiated before it could be made public. The rights of the defense should be respected, and the composition of the tribunal should be carefully selected to ensure impartiality. Evidence should be solid and irrefutable, with no loopholes. Here, however, there is none of this.

I've given hundreds of lectures, lectured thousands of hours, made countless public and media appearances, published countless articles in various newspapers and magazines, been interviewed countless times, taken part in debates—on TV, radio or in associations—aplenty, written nearly sixty books and edited a large number of collective works. I'm extremely active on social networks (Facebook and Twitter). Yet not one line, not one word, not one sentence can corroborate the accusation of anti-Semitism. Not a single complaint on these grounds has been lodged with any court, despite the fact that French legislation is certainly the toughest in the world in the fight against anti-Semitism, and that whistle-blowers and "watchdogs" are legion and particularly responsive. Accusation without proof or motive. Guilty without a crime and convicted without appeal.

Some people are deeply convinced of the relevance of such an accusation, while others obviously know it to be false, but consider it an excellent way of smearing me. The aim is

---

1. See *Die hard 3: A day in hell.*

to disqualify me, to remove me from public debate. How can thousands of my compatriots be sincerely convinced of my anti-Semitism or my hatred of them? Or, to use a recurring expression, of my "Jewish obsession"? None of my actions, none of my writings, none of my words can lend the slightest credence to this thesis. If I find it hard to understand, I must also admit that I haven't always been helped by those whose job it is to reflect, explain and make intelligible what seems confusing. They didn't rush to enlighten me or the public. It's as if they were afraid of suffering, by capillary action, the same opprobrium. As if the evil that afflicted me were highly contagious.

Logically, the subject could—should—have piqued the curiosity of journalists and academics. Indeed, if serious evidence had supported the accusations, they would have stirred up the media sphere. But, on the contrary, the absence of proof and the presumption of innocence did not arouse much interest. This in itself is a profound source of unrest. While I have received many messages of support, no in-depth investigation has been launched... In a democratic country, which claims to be in the vanguard of the promotion of human rights or the philosophy of the Enlightenment, it is appropriate to recall the phrase attributed to Voltaire: "I don't agree with what you say, but I will fight to the death so that you have the right to say it." Wanting to forbid an intellectual to speak and to put to death a research institute because the theses of its director are inconvenient, this should have led to multiple protests, extensive journalistic investigations... But no! Only two articles came in response:

one by Dominique Vidal in Le Monde diplomatique[2] and the other by an Australian academic, Evan Jones (whom I don't know personally), in Counterpunch magazine, following the publication of my book La France malade du conflit israélo-palestinien[3].

"Pascal Boniface is a specialist in what the French call geopolitics. His output has been prodigious, covering a wide variety of subjects. His latest book is entitled La France malade du conflit israélo-palestinien. For his literary efforts in this arena, he has gone from respected commentator to persona non grata in the mainstream media. Rightly obsessed with the promise of universalism officially anchored in the French Republic, he opposes the sabotage of this imperative by those who defend the indefensible policies of Israeli governments, and who hijack and distort politics in France to this end. For his efforts, Pascal Boniface is denigrated and marginalized. Of course, he refuses to admit defeat."

So, how did it come to this? How can a French academic be accused, out of all reality, of one of the most serious intellectual crimes? This book aims to answer these questions.

---

2. Dominique VIDAL, "Au nom du combat contre l'antisémitisme", *Le Monde diplomatique*, December 2002.

3. Evan JONES, "The Israel lobby and French politics", *Counterpunch*, July 9, 2014: https://www.counterpunch.org/2014/07/09/the-israel-lobby-and-french-politics/

You Know Who I am Now

Like many people in France, May '68 had a major influence on my intellectual formation. I wasn't actively involved in the movement—I was in seventh grade, so I was too young to really take part. I had a very vague perception of what it meant and what was at stake. For me, it corresponded to a long period when I was "deprived"—to my great delight—of secondary school. Vacations that came early! My parents were divorced and I lived with my mother and her second husband in Limay, near Mantes-la-Jolie (78). I saw my father every other weekend in Goussainville (95). During the strike, transport was interrupted, so I didn't see my father for several weeks. He didn't have a telephone, which was common in those days. My father-in-law was politically right-wing and supported the government. He was very hostile to the strikers and to student and worker protests. With nothing else to say but these discussions, I spent my time enjoying a vacation that was as welcome as it was unexpected. When transportation was restored, I was able to see my father again. My father had been an active participant in the strike and had a strong left-wing sensibility. I was discovering an opposite version of the same events. From that moment on, I realized that there could be several interpretations of the same event. Always comparing, putting things into perspective, listening to different opinions, became my mantra. I was twelve years old and I haven't changed a single line since.

My middle school years[4] were not brilliant academically, and after barely passing, I had to repeat my ninth year. This was far from a tragedy, as on the one hand I had a year's head start, and on the other hand I was able to approach the second year with more maturity and the beginnings of reflection that failures should always lead to. Two teachers were instrumental in boosting my self-confidence: Claudine Laurent and Jean-Marie Jacqueau. I took advantage of the 1973 legislative elections to organize a debate for high school students, bringing together candidates from all the parties. The debate was contested by the most virulent sections of the extreme left, on the theme of "elections, asshole traps". In the premiere, I created the newspaper Le Censuré, in reference to the Canard enchaîné, of which I had been a faithful reader since May 68. It was quite irreverent, and the principal, Yves de Saint-Do, showed a remarkable tolerance, especially at the time, which I wasn't sufficiently aware of at the time. This experience not only developed my writing skills, but

---

4. I completed my entire secondary education at the Lycée Saint-Exupéry in Mantes-la-Jolie, which at the time was from sixième to terminale.

also my management and organizational skills. In my final year, I became president of the "foyer socio-éducatif" and organized concerts by Gilles Servat, Tri Yann and Joan-Pau Verdier. We managed to break even despite the total absence of subsidies.

I was very active politically. I had joined the Parti socialiste unifié (PSU) in 1973 and was a regular reader of Politique hebdo, which was very much on the left. Three major events marked those formative years:

- In the spring of 1973, all the high schools were up in arms against the Debré law, named after the Minister of Defense, who wanted to reform the deferments granted to students before they did their military service. Young people were profoundly anti-militaristic, not least because of the existence of military service, where bullying outnumbered situational awareness. I was one of the leaders of the high school strike.
- The strike by Lip workers, whose boss wanted to close the plant. The Prime Minister at the time, Pierre Messmer, declared: "Lip, it's over." The workers seized the available stock of watches and sold them to pay themselves, reopening production: "We make, we sell, we pay ourselves." Self-management was underway, we thought. As a PSU activist, I could not help but be enthusiastic, all the more so as Lip's leader, Charles Piaget, was a PSU member. In September 1973, I had taken part in the gigantic, rainy demonstration in Besançon, forging a note of apology from my parents to explain my absence from school.

- On September 11—a decidedly dramatic date—1973, General Augusto Pinochet carried out a bloody coup d'état in Chile, putting an end to Salvador Allende's legal and legitimate People's Union government, just as a Union of the Left was being set up in France with the hope of electoral victory. Pinochet's bloody and violent repression revolted us, and some were worried that this type of scenario could be repeated in France if the parties supporting the common program of the Union of the Left won. The memory of the 1961 Algiers putsch was still vivid, and the Chilean army, hitherto presented as legalistic, had carried out a bloody coup d'état.

Internationally, the struggle against apartheid in South Africa was a powerful mobilizing factor, as was the war in Vietnam and the massive bombing of civilian populations by the US army.

With my A-levels in hand, I enrolled in law school. I would have entered Sciences Po, since politics was my passion, but at the time I thought it was a school for rich kids who didn't have to worry about finding a job. So off I went to law school, where, at the time, I was guaranteed a job. My activism in high school had introduced me to a key figure in Mantes-la-Jolie, Tiennot Grumbach, an advocate of the workers' cause. He fascinated me and I decided to become a lawyer.

I left the PSU in 1974 when the leadership, behind Michel Rocard whom I would later meet again, had rejected the idea of putting Charles Piaget forward for the presidential election, in favor of François Mitterrand in the first round.

My prospects changed after I joined the university, working alongside assistants (teachers who, at the time, taught tutorials, closer to the students than those who lectured), notably Philippe Abella and Christian Merlin. I was drawn to university teaching. I became a part-time day supervisor in my second year, then a full-time one the following year, in order to be financially independent. As I could now only come to the faculty two days a week (the other three days being devoted to my supervisory duties), friends would pass me the notes I'd taken in class. At the time, I was more interested in public law than private law. In my third year, I was introduced to public international law by a brilliant professor, Alain Pellet. If I wasn't able to attend lectures, I attended tutorials in his subject, and then went straight to his teaching in the fourth year and in the DEA (post-graduate diploma)[5]. I found this subject extremely interesting, and closer to politics than the others. Alain Pellet advised me to take a postgraduate course in political science at the Institut d'Etudes Politiques (IEP) in Paris.

Despite a limited number of places—thirty, including fifteen for foreign students—I was accepted, thanks in particular to the breadth of my reading and the knowledge gained from my years of activism. The year was as stimulating as it was uncomfortable. Intellectually, I was opening up to new horizons that fascinated me. Socially, I didn't feel

---

5. Diplôme d'études approfondies, equivalent to today's Master's degree. At the time, the three-year Bachelor's degree was followed by a Master's degree in the fourth year and a DEA in the fifth.

entirely at home, and the fact that, as I was still a "pawn"[6], I couldn't attend all the classes added to my discomfort. To make matters worse, I'd been given a teaching post in constitutional law at Paris XIII, which meant I had to organize myself quite drastically, as I had no intention of leading a monastic life.

During my DEA in public law, Alain Pellet created a course on disarmament, as he and Jean-Pierre Cot were involved in setting up a study and research center on the subject at Paris I University. I wasn't really enthusiastic about the disarmament issue, but he associated me with this center, opening up a new field of interest for me. Having been appointed assistant at Paris XIII, he strongly suggested that I write a thesis on disarmament. After five years of writing[7], I defended it on May 29 1985, the very day of the Heysel tragedy. In 1986, I had the great good fortune to be appointed a senior lecturer and thus a full university professor.

By the early 1980s, I was beginning to specialize in defense and disarmament issues. The election of François Mitterrand left a huge gap in the expertise of the Socialist Party (PS), of which I had become a member, as recognized

---

6. A rather pejorative nickname given to supervisors. I was assigned to the Lycée Marcel Roby in Saint-Germain-en-Laye. I was in charge of a boarding and day school service, which meant I only had to spend two days and one night there, so I gained one day for my studies.

7. Pascal Boniface, *Les sources du droit international de la maîtrise du désarmement*, doctoral thesis defended at the University of Paris Nord Villetaneuse in 1985. A condensed and updated version of this thesis was published under the title *Les sources du désarmement* in 1989 (Éditions Economica).

specialists in international relations were snapped up by ministerial cabinets and parliamentary groups. The strategic news was dense. With the diplomatic battle over the Euromissiles raging on, I was offered a voluntary post: project manager for defense and disarmament issues within the PS's international sector, headed by Jacques Huntzinger. It brought together specialists in major regional areas, and the weekly meetings, where two or three topical issues were discussed, were a source of intellectual enrichment. At the time, the French PS was in the minority in European socialist bodies. Under Mitterrand, France argued for the deployment of American Pershing IIs and cruise missiles, since the USSR was unwilling to withdraw its SS20s. François Mitterrand believed that pressure should be brought to bear to achieve disarmament[8] while most other social-democratic parties, notably the German SPD, militated against the installation of American missiles. It's true that Ronald Reagan, who at the time was talking about the possibility of a limited nuclear war in Europe, didn't inspire much confidence. On the Soviet side, Leonid Brezhnev was counting on the West's division not to give in.

For a Socialist president to advocate the deployment of American nuclear weapons in Europe might seem paradoxical. In any case, it was a position that isolated the

---

8. He advocated "balance from above in order to achieve balance from below". In other words, in the face of the USSR's refusal to unilaterally dismantle its SS20s, he was in favor of deploying American Euromissiles, in order to create a balance that would then lead to mutual disarmament. This is what happened after Gorbachev came to power.

French Socialist Party from the other European Socialist parties. I accompanied J. Huntzinger to meetings which, every four to six weeks, brought together European Socialists to discuss this burning issue. When he couldn't make it, I found myself representing the PS alone, up against the likes of Egon Bahr and Gro Harlem Brundtland. I felt like a dwarf against giants, having to defend ultra-minority positions. It was difficult, but extremely instructive. This voluntary role took up around five or six days a month, and enabled me to continue writing my thesis as well as carrying out my teaching duties at the university. Although the time spent was far from being wasted, I refused to take on any additional paid work until I had finished writing my thesis.

A few weeks after I'd finished the latter, a cataclysm rocked French politics: as a result of the Greenpeace affair[9], Charles Hernu, Minister of Defense, was forced to resign. Jean-François Dubos, one of the Socialist galaxy's leading figures on defense issues and a mentor to me, told me that I needed someone to "mentor" Charles Hernu. I thus became Charles Hernu's assistant, special advisor, pen, chief of staff and director of cabinet, and in fact his main and only collaborator, alongside his loyal secretary, Nicole Constant. The former minister was quite vindictive after his "resignation",

---

9. The *Rainbow Warrior,* a Greenpeace ship campaigning against French nuclear testing, had sunk in the New Zealand port of Auckland following an explosion. One person was killed, and it soon became clear that the explosion was no accident. Two agents of the DGSE (an agency attached to the Ministry of Defense), who had taken part in the operation, were arrested in New Zealand. It was an international scandal.

and we had to make sure that he contained any untimely statements and, above all, that someone was able to feed him with texts, speeches and articles. The plan was for me to accompany him to the 1986 parliamentary elections and then become his parliamentary assistant. Charles Hernu told anyone who would listen that he wouldn't rule out running for president in 1988 if he did well in the parliamentary elections. Although he was not entirely blameless in the Greenpeace affair, many French people saw him as a martyr. He was also a particularly warm-hearted man, who knew how to appeal to the electorate, so much so that he achieved an excellent score in his home department of the Rhône[10], better than that of Raymond Barre, a potential right-wing candidate in the next presidential election. Charles Hernu had also gone from being Minister of Defense, which offers the best logistical facilities, to being a political martyr. As he only had two assistants when he was in Paris, I sometimes had the delicate task of explaining to him that he no longer had quite the same resources as at the Hôtel de Brienne. I had nothing to do with it, but bearers of bad news are rarely popular. Anyway, when he became a Member of Parliament, he didn't keep his promise to take me on as his parliamentary assistant, preferring to recruit his new wife's sister. I was quite distraught at first, but this bad news eventually turned into an opportunity. The position of parliamentary assistant for the Socialist group at the National Assembly became available.

---

10. Elections were then held on the basis of full proportional representation by department.

Pierre Joxe, the group's president, and François Roussely, his chief of staff, took me on. It was an extraordinarily formative period. Under the impetus of these two men, the Socialist Group was remarkably well organized and did a titanic amount of work. The engine of François Mitterrand's future campaign for the 1988 presidential election was underway. I discovered parliamentary work from the inside.

In 1988, Pierre Joxe and Laurent Fabius wanted to know if I wanted to get more directly involved in politics, i.e. run for elected office. It was extremely tempting, I confess. But in the end I declined. I'd seen the work of parliamentarians up close: it's very demanding, even exhausting, and involves countless constraints. While it's true that not all elected representatives give a perfect image of the job, some having long since sacrificed their convictions at the altar of their ambitions, there are still some extremely dedicated people with an overwhelming workload. Many of them have only a few hours a week to themselves, and must multiply evening meetings, weekend inaugurations and smiles for pests. I gave up this prospect to keep control of my schedule and my freedom of speech, and also to preserve my family life. Being an expert, taking part in working groups, playing—at my modest level—on influence rather than power, was more than enough to keep me happy.

In 1985, under the aegis of the Fondation pour les études de Défense nationale (FEDN), I published the first issue of *L'Année stratégique.* It was my first book, an important moment in my career. As its name suggests, this book was to be published every year. But in 1986, just as the second edition was due to come out, Admiral Lacoste was appointed Director of FEDN by the new government. The edition was then postponed until the following year due to "budgetary constraints". This was a pious lie. In truth, I was paying for having been close to Charles Hernu, who had kicked the admiral out of the DGSE before "resigning" from his post as minister. I was extremely bitter about it, but I was still busy with my university activities and the Socialist Group.

In 1988, I joined the cabinet of Jean-Pierre Chevènement, appointed Minister of Defense, as assistant to the diplomatic advisor, Marc Perrin de Brichambaut. Once again, it was a highly formative experience, but at the end of 1989, thinking I'd had enough of the job, I decided to return to academia. I set up the Institut de relations internationales et stratégiques (IRIS) with the primary aim, not of developing a research center, but of creating a legal structure that would enable me to resume publication of L'Année stratégique. This was achieved thanks to a grant of 20,000 francs (around 3,000 euros) given to me by Pierre-Yves Duwoye, J.-P Chevènement's chief of staff. Little did I know that I was about to embark on an adventure that was to leave its mark on my life, as IRIS gradually developed as much by chance as by necessity. Today, it is internationally recognized and regularly ranked highly, especially considering its modest means[11].

So much for my career path.

---

11. See for example: http://www.iris-france.org/communique-de-presse/liris-bon-classement-au-sein-du-global-go-to-think-tanks-2016/

Let's turn to my personal encounter with the issue of anti-Semitism and the Middle East conflict. As far back as I can remember, my first contact with these issues was through a song.

In 1963, Jean Ferrat composed *Nuit et brouillard*, which was an instant hit with audiences of all stripes. It described the horror of the trains that led to death in the concentration camps. At the time, between the desire to forget Vichy and the role the French had played, and the desire to open a new page in relations with Germany, deportation was not a subject that was discussed much. Yet, even as a young child, the song was understandable and gripping. Like many French people of all ages who heard it at the time, it moved me[12].

They were twenty and a hundred, they were thousands
Naked and skinny, trembling, in these leaded wagons
Tearing through the night with their beating nails
They were thousands, they were twenty and a hundred

---

12. In 2005, Meïr Waintrater, director of *l'Arche*, wrote an article in which he explained that this song would now be condemned for implicit Holocaust denial. Indeed, Jean Ferrat sang: "Their names were Jean-Pierre, Natacha or Samuel/Some prayed to Jesus, Jehovah or Vishnu/Others didn't pray, but who cares about heaven/They just wanted to stop living on their knees [...]." There was only one Jewish first name in three, which did not correspond in proportion to the number of Jewish victims of the concentration camps. Jean Ferrat, who was Jewish himself and whose father had been deported, was particularly outraged by this attack, wondering whether such remarks were not simply the stuff of psychiatry.

And to mark his desire to pass on to younger generations, Jean Ferrat continued:

I'd twist words if I had to twist them
So that one day children will know who you were

In 1967, Salvatore Adamo—then at the height of his fame—sang *Inch'Allah*, which reinforced pro-Israeli sentiments after the Six-Day War.

God of hell or God of heaven
You can find yourself wherever you want
On this land of Israel
There are children who tremble
Inch'Allah Inch'Allah Inch'Allah Inch'Allah
[...]
Requiem for six million souls
Who do not have their marble mausoleum
And despite the infamous sand
Grew six million trees
Inch'Allah Inch'Allah Inch'Allah Inch'Allah "

My passion for Léo Ferré had also led me to discover, as a teenager, *L'Affiche rouge*. So I found out about the FTP-MOI (Francs-tireurs et partisans—Main-d'œuvre immigrée). These foreigners (and brothers), most of them Jewish, had fought in the Resistance[13].

---

13. Little did I know then that I would later have the pleasure of forming a personal bond with one of them, André Schmer—whom I met when our mutual friend Jean-Claude Lefort was awarded the Légion d'honneur—and who subsequently did me the friendship and honor of presenting him with the Légion d'honneur when it was finally awarded to him.

When I entered the Saint-Exupéry secondary school in Mantes-la-Jolie at the age of ten, there were practically no Arabs. In fact, they didn't go to the "classic" lycée, but rather to a technical school where they could learn manual trades. There were Jews, but none of them identified themselves or claimed to be Jewish. If they assumed it, they didn't feel the need to affirm it. In sixth and seventh grade, my best friend was Jewish. I know that "every anti-Semite has a Jewish friend", but I didn't find out about his identity until much later.

After May '68, when I began to take a close interest in current affairs, I was a posteriori seduced by the slogan "We are all German Jews", in solidarity with Daniel Cohn-Bendit. In the eighth grade, I attended a high school screening of *Nuit et Brouillard* (1965), Alain Resnais's documentary on the concentration camps. The weight of the unbearable images had a profound effect on me. That same year, I was also deeply affected by reading Anne Frank's diary and Arthur Koestler's novel *Ezra's Tower*, which gave an extremely positive account of the brave, sympathetic Jewish pioneers who settled in Palestine in the face of hostile, unsympathetic and violent Arabs. At the beginning of the 1970s, the Vichy regime's responsibility was being discussed, and the horrors of Nazism were regularly evoked. A television documentary-drama on the Dreyfus Affair highlighted the nobility of the fight against anti-Semitism. The documentary *Le Chagrin et la Pitié* highlighted the horrors of the Collaboration, buried in the depths of collective memory.

I was therefore very strongly sensitized to the cause of combating anti-Semitism. The abominable horrors of the concentration camps, the hunt for Jews under the Vichy regime, the unbearable injustice of the Dreyfus affair, as well as admiration for the great Jewish thinkers who had advanced knowledge and understanding, were all elements that engendered a natural sympathy for Jews.

In 1978, I decided to leave the suburbs and move to Paris. I found lodgings on rue des Écouffes, in the Marais district, at a time when the area was still extremely popular. The deep-rooted identity of this Jewish neighborhood (which nevertheless did not prevent the difference between Ashkenazim and Sephardim who arrived in the early 1960s) was in no way incompatible with openness to goyim. Quite the contrary, in fact. I was warmly welcomed in this neighborhood, where I lived happily from 1978 to 1985. The Rue des Rosiers bombing (1982), however, created a rift. Under the pretext of ensuring security, community militias, often made up of young radicals, were set up, without any reaction from the public authorities. Assuming the right to maintain order, they did not hesitate to open the bags, sometimes ruthlessly, not only of those passing through, but also of non-Jewish residents, convinced that they were in the right. That's when I started hearing arguments like: "You can't understand," or: "You're not like us." In short, an asserted and claimed distinction between neighbors, depending on whether they were Jewish or not. The Lebanon war would later amplify this divide.

My assessment of the Israeli-Palestinian conflict has evolved over the years in a way that, it seems to me, is fairly representative of the general and global evolution of French public opinion: from strong support for Israel to awareness of the plight of the Palestinians. However, I happen to be more involved professionally than the average French citizen, and have paid a particular price for my public stance on the subject.

I first heard about the conflict during the Six-Day War. I was eleven years old and in the sixth grade. At the time, I was following the general opinion of the French and the media on the subject: a small, courageous people was being attacked by Arabs, who were more numerous, violent and uncivilized. The survivors of the Shoah had succeeded in making the desert bloom, something the Arabs had previously been unable to do. Most of the French media sided overwhelmingly with Israel, as the Arabs had (already) bad press. The Arabs were even portrayed as aggressors, beyond all reality. The Israeli victory was widely hailed, almost a vicarious source of pride. The scale of the Arab defeat was seen as the manifestation of immanent justice. General de Gaulle's decision to impose a partial arms embargo on Israel went against public opinion. Shortly afterwards, during the Cherbourg speedboat affair— on Christmas night 1969—when Israel took possession of the ships initially destined for it but blocked by the embargo, the press and public opinion hailed this feat, which nonetheless ridiculed France. When President Georges Pompidou was attacked by Chicago's Jewish community for selling arms to Arab countries, again most of the French media were in step with the American demonstrators.

Naturally, I was appalled by the attack on the Israeli delegation at the 1972 Munich Olympics, and could not understand why unarmed athletes were targeted.

The Yom Kippur War (unanimously referred to as such in the Western world, but referred to as the "Ramadan War" in Arab countries) attracted less debate and attention, even though I was older and able to keep up with current events. It's true that it had ended on a kind of strategic limb[14] and that, above all, other international events had attracted attention. In the 1970s, the Israeli-Palestinian conflict was drowned in the strategic headlines. Compared with other international events, it did not come to the fore.

I had mixed feelings about the 1978 Camp David Accords and the Egyptian-Israeli peace. While the signing of a peace agreement could only be welcomed, at the same time I sensed that Egypt had gone it alone in breaking Arab solidarity (and I had no taste for those who, to gain personal advantage, break existing bonds of solidarity) and that the rights of the Palestinians had more or less been written off. But I had my doubts. Wasn't Anwar Sadat's bold initiative going to break the deadlock? Wasn't he the visionary who knew how to break with his own people in the name of the common good? Unfortunately, this was not to be.

The 1982 Lebanon war created a different climate. Israel was clearly the aggressor, and had also attacked civilian populations. The "David versus Goliath" aspect was no longer in play. While the Israeli army cannot be

---

14. In chess, when a player—whose turn it is to play and whose king is not in check—is unable to make a valid move and cannot move his king without being put in check, the king is said to be stalemated, regardless of the advantage of pieces or position on either side. The game is then declared a draw.

directly blamed for the massacre at Sabra and Chatila[15], it was nonetheless a silent accomplice. But the opprobrium heaped on the Israeli state was offset by the respect due to the Peace Now movement. It was gratifying to see the vigour of Israeli civil society, capable of challenging its own leaders in the name of universal values. The first Intifada (1987-1993) caused a further deterioration in Israel's image, as it was no longer confronted by stubborn autocrats but by teenagers expressing their rage at being occupied and repressed.

The signing of the Oslo Accords in 1993 was an unexpected shock that ushered in a period of optimism rarely seen. To say that this agreement filled me with joy would be an understatement. I sincerely believed that once the peace agreement had been signed and Yitzhak Rabin, Shimon Peres and Yasser Arafat had shaken hands, there would be no turning back of the wheel of history. Real, definitive peace was about to arrive. Some remained cautious, speaking of the asymmetry of the situations. Israel had recognized the PLO, and the Palestinians the State of Israel. Palestinian territory was divided into three zones. It was believed that the creation of a virtuous circle would gradually sweep away these obstacles.

As a teacher at Paris XIII, I was also struck by the attitude of the students. Historically, Villetaneuse has been the faculty of diversity, ensuring the social advancement of the inhabitants

---

15. Palestinian fighters withdrew from both camps, leaving women, children and the elderly defenseless. Christian militias took advantage of the situation to carry out a massacre, which the nearby Israeli army allowed to happen.

of the 93 region. The Union des étudiants juifs de France (UEJF) was well established and SOS Racisme was born here. But as time went on, students' attitudes to the Israeli-Palestinian conflict changed. In the early 1980s, when I began my teaching career, most Jewish students were unwavering in their solidarity with Israel. Arab students, on the other hand, were overwhelmingly in favor of the Palestinians. The rest were evenly divided between the two. Twenty years later, most of the students, who were neither Jewish nor Arab, placed the main burden of responsibility for the conflict on Israel. There was a widely shared sense of injustice, of a double standard, and of abnormal treatment of the conflict.

I'm not telling you this story to show off my life, which is nothing out of the ordinary. In fact, I believe it to be representative of how most French people perceive the Israeli-Palestinian conflict. I'm doing this to demonstrate the consistency of my commitment to justice, freedom and respect for others. I have never accepted hypocrisy, lies and compromises to gain advantages. These are the reasons that led me to speak out against the Israeli government's occupation of Palestine and its people. I'm glad that I've remained true to my rebellious adolescent commitments, and that maturity hasn't hampered my desire and strength to denounce injustice wherever it may be, even if sometimes at great cost[16].

---

16. I'm particularly proud that the teaching staff at the Lycée Saint-Exupéry in Mantes-la-Jolie, led by Nathalie Coste, asked me to act as "godfather" to the students preparing for the Sciences Po entrance exam thanks to the priority education agreements.

The Letter

In 2000, Alain Chenal, in charge of the Middle East/ Mediterranean sector at the SP's international secretariat, announced to me that a small working group was to be set up to consider a new SP position on the Israeli-Palestinian conflict, in view of the ambiguity of recent years. In reality, the SP didn't want to think too much about the issue, and even less about raising sensitive questions[17]. With the failure of the Camp David summit heralding the failure of the Oslo process, the SP was deeply divided, and it was difficult to organize a debate on the subject without provoking strong emotional reactions from those close to Israel. Existing links with the Israeli Labor Party dated back to the French Section of the Workers' International (SFIO), but also, more broadly, to the Israeli establishment. The PS wanted to break with the legacy

---

17. At the international secretariat, there was a manager with special responsibility for Israel. Israel was therefore treated as a special case.

of the SFIO, the proximity that had led—against the backdrop of the Algerian war—to the disastrous Franco-British military intervention in Suez in 1956. The PS leadership could be summarily considered more pro-Israeli than the rank and file. It was made up of leaders who belonged to the Jewish community and were in fusion with Israel (universalist Jews being in the minority), non-Jews who strongly supported Israel in the name of Western solidarity or the defense of the democratic camp, and others who were indifferent and just wanted to avoid any problems. They understood that the best way to avoid getting into trouble was to refrain from any criticism (of the Israeli government) likely to provoke more lightning than that of the opposite camp. The few Arab members of the SP generally avoided expressing themselves on this subject. Too strong an expression on their part would have relegated them to the ranks of anti-Semites and/or communitarians. I often heard them say: "You know, since I'm Arab, I can't really express myself on this subject." I've never heard a Jew make such a remark.

President Mitterrand's policy prevented the PS from reverting to the "mollétist" prism of the Fourth Republic, and could thus be seen as much more active in favor of a settlement than in maintaining the status quo, and thus opposed to the Israeli occupation. The man who had been seen as highly pro-Israeli and philosemitic, and whose election had greatly alarmed the Arab world in 1981, pursued a policy as President that was insensitive to national community pressures and driven solely by France's desire for influence. This led him, in 1982, to become the first French president to visit Israel, delivering a speech to the Knesset in which he spoke of the Palestinians' right to a state: "This right [to live] is yours. It is that of the peoples around you. And I am thinking, of course, of the Palestinians of Gaza and the West Bank. He affirmed his wish that "[...] the Arab inhabitants of the West Bank and Gaza should have a homeland". Finally, he declared: "Dialogue presupposes that each side can pursue its rights to the end, which for the Palestinians as for others may, in due course, mean a state."

What's more, François Mitterrand felt that the representative of a people could not be appointed in its stead, and that Yasser Arafat, regarded by the Israelis and most Westerners as a terrorist, clearly enjoyed the almost unanimous support of the Palestinian people. It was therefore with him that the Israelis should negotiate peace, if they really wanted it, and not with Palestinians of their own choosing. He also supported Arafat in 1982, when the latter was surrounded by the Israeli army in Beirut and some in Tel Aviv were planning to eliminate him physically. He supported Arafat a second time when Syrian President Hafez al-Assad wanted to get rid of the Palestinian leader.

In 1989, despite protests from representatives of the Jewish community at what they saw as the reception of a terrorist, he agreed to Yasser Arafat's visit to Paris. The French Socialist Party (PS), which had fallen behind François Mitterrand's positions, was nevertheless in no position to contest them. While Israel's staunchest supporters grumbled, they could not openly express their opposition. Once François Mitterrand had left the Élysée Palace, the latter regained hope of regaining the upper hand. It's true that Lionel Jospin, who became head of the French Socialist Party after his defeat in the 1995 presidential election, was a determined supporter of Israel, even though he was not Jewish. In the 1980s, he even called for the transfer of the French embassy from Tel Aviv to Jerusalem. In his view, Israel was a democratic country fighting against the dictatorships that surrounded it. As a member of the Socialist International, he had rubbed shoulders with Israeli leaders and felt guilty about anti-Semitism and the Holocaust. Paradoxically, it was his disastrous trip to Bir Zeit in February 2000 that changed his mind[18]. Although he was greeted by stone-throwing at the Palestinian university, he realized that his pro-Israeli entourage had prepared the trip poorly and had misinformed him. He became aware of what Palestinians were going through under occupation.

So I took part in this working group as a generalist on strategic issues, and by no means as a specialist on the Middle East. But it was certainly because I was freeing myself from the constraints, the framework of thought and understanding to which specialists in a subject are accustomed, that I brought a somewhat different perspective.

---

18. Palestinian students criticized Lionel Jospin for describing the Lebanese Hezbollah as a "terrorist movement", whereas they considered it to be a movement of resistance to Israel. They pelted him with stones, and Jospin had to be exfiltrated by his security service. President Jacques Chirac (we were in a period of cohabitation) took the opportunity to call him to order.

We had just emerged from the war in Kosovo, which had itself put an end to the Balkan wars of the 1990s. Despite my closeness to the ruling Socialist Party and to Prime Minister Jospin, Hubert Védrine, Minister of Foreign Affairs, and Alain Richard, Minister of Defense, I was uncomfortable with France's official position. Bombing a country without a UN green light seemed to me not only contrary to international law, but also to our diplomatic principles and our status as a permanent member of the Security Council. During the Balkan wars, I had been somewhat annoyed by the moral posturing of some, summing up this conflict as a position between good and evil, presenting the Serbs as neo-Nazis and the other protagonists as white doves. Although I felt that Milosevic was primarily responsible, I didn't think that the other Balkan leaders could be exonerated. We later learned of the role played by communications agencies in shaping opinion on this conflict. I also found it curious that we could protest against the ethnic cleansing carried out by the Serbs without doing the same for that which had been carried out to their detriment, particularly with regard to those living before 1999 in Kosovo and in 1995 in Croatia. Some of the most outspoken advocates of the Kosovar cause were also avowed supporters of Israel. I found it intellectually contradictory to demand that the right of peoples to self-determination should apply in the case of Kosovo and not to the Palestinians. The Kosovo war was in fact a precursor to the 2003 Iraq war, which France opposed with flamboyance. An illegal war, waged in the name of universal principles hypocritically put forward and poorly concealing strategic interests: geopolitical control of the Middle East in 2003, the need to prove that, fifty years after its creation and ten years after the fall of the Wall, the NATO of 1999 was still useful. Why, when Yugoslavia's sovereignty over Kosovo was not officially called into question, was it bombed? Why was Yugoslavia asked, before the war, to accept the deployment of NATO troops on its territory? And why, when we don't recognize Israel's sovereignty over Palestine, have we not only never bombed Israel, but even voted for the slightest sanction against it? And, of course, we have never called for the deployment of foreign troops, even if only in the illegally occupied territories, to protect the civilian population.

I was also struck by the contradiction between the vigor of the fight against the extreme right in France and Europe, and the total silence in the face of the extreme statements made by certain Israeli leaders. It was as if the fact of being Israeli meant that all political criticism was exonerated, even in the most excessive cases. Ariel Sharon had returned to power in Israel, and it was hard to understand why the PS did not distance itself from him[19]. It's true that the Israeli Labor Party had become the junior partner in the government coalition. And every time I asked out loud why the universal principles that the SP, the left in general and even the right claimed to uphold didn't apply to the Middle East conflict, I received the same embarrassed answers: "it's more complicated", "it's different, there's a whole history to take into account". The past,

---

19. In 2002, I heard one of the heads of the Israel sector describe him as "a bulwark against Benyamin Netanyahu"!

but also the internal balances within the PS, the number of militants with varying degrees of attachment to Israel, the link that still exists in people's minds between criticism of Israel and anti-Semitism, prevented us from treating the Israeli-Palestinian conflict like any other conflict. Electoral issues, more intuitive than well-founded, also came to the fore.

While there was no such thing as a specific Jewish vote, throughout the 1970s, members of the French Jewish community mobilized more strongly in favor of Israel. In 1981, it seemed established that French Jews were more likely to vote for Mitterrand than for Giscard d'Estaing. The Left was supposed to fight anti-Semitism more than the Right. Giscard was accused of not being sufficiently favorable to Israel, and of having been one of the initiators, within the European Economic Community (EEC), of the 1980 Venice Declaration recognizing Palestinian rights. Never mentioned publicly, often in private, the "Jewish vote" was well and truly taken into account by many officials on the basis of intuitions or statements by personalities often unrepresentative of the diversity of the French Jewish community.

This contradiction is all the more important when you claim to be a leftist, for two reasons. The first reason is that the Left has always supported the development of law to pacify international relations, believing that it was better for international relations to be governed by international law rather than by force. In the case of the Israeli-Palestinian question, however, it was force that prevailed. International law, which condemns the acquisition of territory by military force and forbids recourse to war, has been flouted since 1967, and a binding Security Council resolution calling for the return of the occupied territories has never been implemented. The various UN resolutions have piled up in vain, and the Geneva Conventions governing the fate of populations facing military occupation are flouted on a daily basis. The second reason is that I find it extremely difficult to call oneself a leftist while accepting the principle of the occupation of one people by another, with all the consequences in terms of repression that this implies... A military occupation brings repression like the cloud brings the storm.

It was unnatural for the PS to remain silent in the face of Ariel Sharon's actions. In particular, it was forgetting Sharon's moral responsibility for demonizing Yitzhak Rabin, which led to his assassination. It's no coincidence that his widow, Lea, subsequently refused to shake hands with Sharon and Netanyahu[20]. Sharon had always opposed the Oslo process and had announced loud and clear that he intended to dismantle it. There was therefore no objective reason for the SP not to condemn him.

Without saying so publicly, many Socialist leaders advocated immobilism, for fear of both awakening the demons of anti-Semitism and suffering the negative electoral fallout. Always think about it, never talk about it, seemed to be the central thought of many leaders in relation to the Israeli-Palestinian conflict and its consequences for the French Jewish vote. What's more, the municipal elections were

---

20. It's quite symptomatic that the Bercy garden, dedicated to Yitzhak Rabin, mentions his assassination but doesn't specify the perpetrator, as if it were a crime without a criminal.

approaching, and the "Jewish vote" was seen as "crucial" to the PS's future conquest of Paris. The argument used by many was precisely electoral: don't frighten the "Jewish vote", don't frighten "the community".

On the basis of these reflections, I wrote a note to Henri Nallet[21], International Secretary of the French Socialist Party, and to François Hollande, who was its First Secretary. I could never have imagined the impact it would have on my personal and professional life. The note began to circulate. The most ardent supporters of Israel within the PS circulated it intensively to denounce its danger. They were worried, fearing a change in the SP's line on the subject.

---

21. See Appendix 1.

Damnation

From the beginning of May 2001, I began receiving e-mails from Israel counter-arguing my note that had leaked there, sometimes courteously, but also more sharply, even insultingly. In July, I decided to write an article about it, which I sent to Le *Monde.* At the time, I had no problem publishing in the columns of this daily[22]. This was not to be the case thereafter. The article was published on August 4, and I thought it was a pity that it was published in the middle of summer, when attention is at its lowest. How wrong I was! One of my former students, Alexandre Tuaillon, whose talent I had noticed at the IEP in Lille where I was teaching at the

---

22. This was not to be the case thereafter. In a book published in 2003 by Robert Laffont, *Une histoire personnelle de l'antisémitisme,* Nicolas Weill, long in charge of the "Ideas" section at Le *Monde, was* able to write a chapter entitled "De Roger Garaudy à Pascal Boniface" (From Roger Garaudy to Pascal Boniface), without shocking many people. He then successfully tried to block my access to the daily news.

time, had just taken up his post at IRIS, as head of communications. Before going on vacation myself, I told him that it was a quiet period and that he would have a smooth start. Once again, what a huge error of judgement!

On August 8, *Le Monde* published, this time on its front page, an article by the Israeli ambassador to France, Élie Barnavi. Barnavi lashed out violently at me, calling into question my article and my internal PS memo. By its very existence, this article should have raised eyebrows. Could an ambassador from a foreign country other than Israel have published such a virulent article against a French intellectual who had criticized his government, accusing him of racism, on the front page of what was then the "reference" daily of the French intelligentsia? Wouldn't it rather have been unanimously opposed to this attempt at foreign interference in the French debate and obstruction of freedom of expression? In any case, *Le Monde* would not have published it on its front page. It wrote that behind my tendentious presentation of the facts lay a desire to "delegitimize the State of Israel", and that I had produced "frank and hateful anti-Israeli language bordering on anti-Semitism"[23]. Delegitimizing the State of Israel was to become a recurring argument against all those who criticized its government. Saying that someone is "borderline anti-Semitic" is a way of smearing him or her while avoiding being sued for libel. It's clever if not correct. The fact that the attack came from Élie Barnavi added to

---

23. With a slight misrepresentation of historical reality, he asserted that the Six-Day War had been provoked by Egypt's aggressiveness, whereas Israel had indeed initiated it, playing on the element of surprise.

its weight. Before being appointed Israel's ambassador to France by Ehud Barak's Labor government, he was a moral and intellectual figure on the Israeli left. A historian with an imposing and recognized body of work, a supporter of peace with the Palestinians, he knew how to charm audiences. So I was attacked not by someone from the hard right, but by a left-wing intellectual. Since his appointment as ambassador, which, given his profile, offered him a central place in Parisian life, the Israeli government had changed. Ariel Sharon, who had always opposed peace with the Palestinians, had taken the helm. In a historic mistake, the Labor Party had agreed to take part in the government as a minority, in order to retain a few positions and material advantages, and this was to be the signal for their political decline to the disastrous state to which this founding party of the State of Israel has now been reduced. Élie Barnavi certainly acted on instructions from Tel Aviv, having no other choice if he wanted to keep his job than to indulge in this baseness towards me. Israel was under fire, France was an important country and the position of ambassador there was highly enviable. Much later, Barnavi, no longer an ambassador, returned to other feelings and made comments about the Israeli government that were far more violent than those contained in either my note or my article, more than roundly reproaching it on numerous occasions for opposing peace.

But, at the time, he was ambassador to Ariel Sharon, then Prime Minister. His article was so violent that Claude, the friend I was staying with on vacation in Aix-en-Provence, asked me what I could have written to trigger such a thunderbolt. He was worried that my pen might have slipped. I had to show him my initial article to get him to admit that the violence of Barnavi's attack was unjustified.

I'd had the misfortune to bring my laptop with me. I was immediately assailed by messages of protest, recrimination, insults and even threats—the hunt was on! I tried to reply when the tone wasn't too violent. It was painful to be accused of anti-Semitism, and I tried—sometimes successfully, but often in vain—to convince my interlocutors that the accusation was unfounded. The IRIS switchboard was stormed, most of the time by people who had nothing but insults on their lips, and were collectively punishing the unfortunate collaborator Alexandre Tuaillon, who was not supposed to be responsible for my actions. Anger seemed to prevent any reflection. By e-mail or letter, messages arrived by the hundreds: virulent criticism, insults and even death threats.

I did my best to keep my family out of it, whose support and comfort were precious to me, but who didn't have to suffer these torments. It was very difficult, given the public nature of the controversy. I didn't keep her informed of the most hateful messages, so as not to add to her worries. Unfortunately, this wasn't always possible when death threats were delivered directly to my mailbox.

I also received many messages of congratulations, encouragement and support for having said things that many people thought but few expressed publicly, and that we hardly ever had the opportunity to read.

Specific messages were addressed to the Jewish members of the IRIS board, showing the ultra-communitarian vision of those who sent them. They were asked to make up their minds as Jews.

On August 6, 2001, Clément Weill-Raynal, then president of the Association des Journalistes Juifs de France—whose members could be counted on the fingers of one hand—wrote a letter to Serge Weinberg, chairman of the IRIS board of directors, co-signed by lawyer Gilles-William Goldnadel, in which he wrote: "[The note] has caused a stir within the Jewish community, which has thus found itself collectively called into question and denied the legitimate right to support Israel within the framework of democratic debate." I was accused of "[…] holding the Jewish community responsible in advance for a new wave of anti-Semitism that could strike it if it did not agree to collectively repent." He added: "If we accept his peremptory arguments, such outbursts can only be detrimental to IRIS's reputation on the Board of Directors on which you sit. We also know that we have always been able to count you among the friends of Israel in France. It is for these reasons that we wanted to share our emotions with you, and we hope that they will be echoed by IRIS's governing bodies".

If pro-Palestinian associations had written to the management of France 3, where journalist Weill-Raynal worked (albeit very moderately, due to his community activities, notably as a contributor to the magazine *Actualité juive*, in which he wrote articles under a pseudonym), to complain about his militant activity and his numerous slip-ups, there is no doubt that this would have created an outcry against this intolerable attack on freedom of expression.

Clément Weill-Raynal addresses Serge Weinberg as a member of the Jewish community. What's more, he is writing directly to my superior without any prior direct contact with me. Finally, he finds it normal to support Israel as part of a democratic debate, but inadmissible to criticize it.

I then met his twin brother Guillaume. In 2004, Guillaume published a formidable and courageous book, Une haine imaginaire? Contre-enquête sur le nouvel antisémitisme (An imaginary hatred? A counter-inquiry into the new anti-Semitism), in which he demonstrated that anti-Semitism had increased exponentially after 2000. The press boycotted this book, which challenged widely-held preconceptions and, above all, denounced the thesis of the rise in anti-Semitism, a thesis that the press itself had spread and which was very much in vogue in the media. Yet there would have been a fascinating subject: twin brothers at opposite ends of the spectrum, one ultra-communitarian, i.e. systematically supporting Israel, whatever its policies and behavior, out of community solidarity, and the other fiercely universalist, i.e. judging actors according to universal principles and not according to their community identities. It would have been a good way to combat anti-Semitism and show the diversity of Jewish appreciation of the Israeli-Palestinian conflict, which could even go so far as to pit twins against each other! But no. Most of the media preferred not to confront the thesis of official Jewish institutions.

Thereafter, Clément Weill-Raynal regularly attacked me, each time referring to me as "the very anti-Israeli Boniface". I pointed out that my position was the same as that of many

Israelis in favor of an agreement with the Palestinians, and that the same debate was taking place within Israeli society. Did he mean that being in favor of a two-state solution was an anti-Israeli position? He was confusing anti-Likud with anti-Israel...

He was at it again in 2008. I accompanied a group from Terre entière, a tour operator with close ties to Christian circles, on a trip to Lebanon. It was the first time an organized tour had taken French people to Lebanon since the 2006 war. We saw all the components of Lebanese political life represented in Parliament before embarking on a trip to this wonderful country. Among our various meetings was one with members of Hezbollah. Clément Weill-Raynal ran an article in *Actualité juive* explaining that I had gone to Lebanon specifically to meet Hezbollah, while remaining silent about my many other contacts. Here again, a formidable manipulation of the facts: in a particularly fiendish fashion, he claimed to possess photos of the meeting, as if he were in a position to reveal a fact that I had carefully concealed. The readers of *Actualité juive* could not have known that all the photos of the stay and the meetings had been published on the Terre entière website where he had found them. The fact that I had befriended his brother Guillaume had increased his hostility towards me.

On August 13, 2001, *Le Monde* published an article by lawyer Pierre-François Veil criticizing me for "threatening to ban the French Jewish community from the national community for collective offence of opinion". Six days later, in another article, Roland Bechmann criticized Élie Barnavi for ignoring the problem of Jewish settlements in the occupied territories: "Jews, or those classified as such, who lived through the Occupation in France and who, like me, joined the Resistance, cannot approve of such a policy leading to an inevitable catastrophe. And I don't think that the majority of members of France's heterogeneous Jewish community, when questioned individually, would agree. This is not only because it feeds anti-Semitism, from which they may have to suffer, but simply because it runs counter to the values of tolerance, respect for human rights, democracy and openness that have long made France a pole of attraction for many people from foreign countries."

These two contributions illustrate the type of message I was receiving, diametrically opposed, strong support and vigorous accusations, from Jews and non-Jews alike. They also showed that the debate—the fight—is not between Jews and non-Jews, but between universalists and communitarian Jews.

I had set myself the guideline of responding systematically, when there was no insult or threat, and of maintaining a dialogue. This is how I came to take part in a debate organized by Sylvain Attal on RMC info, with Élie Barnavi. As a teacher at the IEP in Lille at the time, I took the opportunity to invite the ambassador to give a talk to the students, which he accepted to my great satisfaction. In an amphitheatre packed to the rafters, he gave a talk that will live long in the memory of those who attended[24]. Only one spectator in the

---

24. Shortly afterwards, I organized a similar conference with Leïla Shahid, Palestine's representative in Paris. She also made a strong impression, so much so that the students at IEP wanted to name their class after her. The IEP management opposed the idea, fearing the problems it might cause.

front row didn't seem to share the audience's satisfaction. At the friendly drink that followed, I approached him. It was the regional representative of the Conseil représentatif des institutions juives de France (CRIF), who declared, all anger misplaced, that he'd come to the conference because he couldn't do otherwise—since the Israeli ambassador was there—but that he was shocked that I could host it after my August article. Once again, I tried to explain the accusation of anti-Semitism and indicated my availability for any debate or discussion. This set him off and he launched into a long, confused and aggressive monologue, while Élie Barnavi looked on, stunned and embarrassed by such stupidity.

It wasn't long before support began to emerge that I quickly dismissed. People who come to you or send you messages assuring you of their support are always comforting, except when you understand their real intentions. Some tell you that you're right, that the Jews control everything, that they're wholeheartedly with you in the fight against their influence... In short, real anti-Semites surrounded me with their solicitude. I immediately made it clear to them that I didn't share their views and that I refused to mix things up.

For, in fact, while I was besieged, I was also surrounded by real and honorable supporters. Invited to the PS summer university at the end of August 2001, *Le Monde* had just published my response to Élie Barnavi. On the train to La Rochelle, I was regarded as a pest by some (including people who knew me well but didn't want to take the risk of being seen with me) and received encouragement and warm greetings from comrades I didn't know.

When I arrived at the Encan space in La Rochelle, where the summer university was being held, Jean-Michel Rosenfeld, who was very close to Pierre Mauroy, ostentatiously gave me a hug, showing that he was not part of the pack. I was to take part in a round table discussion. I learned that a few excited people were ready to come and not only mess up the room, but also push me around quite badly. Some of their friends explained to them that this was not an excellent idea for their own interests. Warned of what was going on, other people came along, ready to defend me if anything went wrong. In the end, nothing happened. At dinner, a group of young socialists came up to me to say that their hearts went out to me, and that they were pleased that the SP was finally expressing itself in this way. They thanked me for expressing what they felt without having the opportunity to do so. Back in Paris, I received a phone call shortly afterwards from Pascal Cherki, whom I knew a little since he was Bertrand Delanoë's deputy sports director. He offered to meet me for lunch, and said he would come and invite me. He couldn't understand how anyone could call himself a Jew and treat me like that. Michel Dreyfus-Schmidt, while I was being heard by a Senate committee to which he did not belong, burst into the room where the meeting was being held to greet me and, in full view of everyone, express his rejection of the witch trial and his solidarity with me. Henri Israël, editor-in-chief of *CFDT Magazine*, also lent me his support.

A student in charge of the national office of the Union des étudiants juifs de France (UEJF), Paul Bernard, contacted me. I was delighted at the idea of an exchange that would build bridges and dispel misunderstandings. He came with one of his fellow students and we had a long discussion at IRIS, during which we exchanged agreements and disagreements in an open and serene manner, and during which he asked me to come to Marseille to debate with students from his organization. Paul Bernard, though attached to his Jewish identity and to Israel, was a man of dialogue. Alas, he must have been isolated in his willingness to engage in dialogue, for due to reluctance within his association, the debate was never organized.

In an article published in *Le Monde* on September 6, 2001, Théo Klein, Honorary President of CRIF, recognized that Israel's current policy of repression could only lead to disaster. He called on Ariel Sharon to immediately recognize the Palestinian state and demanded the partition of Jerusalem, even going so far as to assert that a terrorist supported by his people became a combatant. His moral stance was in line with his conception of Judaism and his support for Israel. This article showed, if proof were needed, that opposition to the policy pursued by the Israeli government could in no way be equated with anti-Semitism or opposition to Israel's existence.

All this shows, if proof were needed, the diversity of the Jewish community. It's not the Jews who have attacked me. It's some of them, for their own reasons. And there is a cleavage, not between Jews and others, but between communitarians and universalists.

L'Arche magazine, the official organ of the institution-alized Jewish community, devoted a long, accusatory dossier to me in September 2001[25]. It portrayed me as dangerous—voluntarily or involuntarily—for the Jews of France. Le journal du judaïsme called the article by its editor-in-chief Meïr Waintrater: "Docteur Pascal, Mister Boniface". Serge Weinberg, in a right of reply published in the January-February 2002 issue, declared that he found the accusations levelled against me unbearable, as they were totally contrary to reality, and that he could vouch for one essential point: my constant commitment to fighting racism and anti-Semitism. He went on to say that the accusation of anti-Semitism was "too serious to be made lightly, and that he felt that in these days, even more than in the past, it was often used as an argument to disqualify ideas or positions deemed by some to be contrary to Israel's interests, without accepting the necessary dialogue". He went on to write that "the effect was simply to encourage people to turn in on themselves". Serge Weinberg was expressing himself for the first time as a Jew, because this part of his identity could not, in his view, sum up who he was. He also told me that he was dismayed to discover that there were fascists among the Jews.

The December 6, 2001 issue of *L'Express* and the December 7, 2001 issue of *Valeurs actuelles* each published a relatively similar dossier. Not surprising, since the source, although not cited by the weeklies, was the same: the CRIF.

Under the pen of Éric Conan, *L'Express* published "Les chiffres noirs de l'antisémitisme" ("The black figures of

---

25. After the publication of my book *Est-il permis de critiquer Israël*, *I received* two other dossiers in April and September 2003.

anti-Semitism"). The article featured photos of burnt-out synagogues, and pointed to an increase in the number of attacks on Jews perpetrated by young people from Arab-Muslim immigrant families.

"When there are five or six million Muslims in France and only six hundred thousand Jews, it's clear that the Muslim community is better taken into account," declared Chief Rabbi Sitruk [...] "It's true that a recent incident within the PS fosters this fear. Pascal Boniface, a member of the PS and director of IRIS, suggested at a closed meeting of the party's international commission that it would be more profitable, in order to take into account the votes of the Arab-Muslim community in 2002, to modify the official policy towards Israel."

My right of reply will be published in the "Courrier de lecteurs" under the rather un-neutral title: "A new anti-Semitism?" The least we can say is that this was not the most ethical way of going about things.

Éric Conan, decidedly relentless against me, even called me into question four times in the space of ten months in the columns of *L'Express*. When I pointed out to him, during a telephone conversation, that he was distorting my thoughts, he replied: "Yes, but that's not how your note is interpreted within the community." A fine example of journalistic rigor!

In the May 22-28, 2003 issue of *L'Express*, Alfred Grosser published a glowing review of my book *Est-il permis de critiquer Israël?* Do I need to introduce Alfred Grosser? One of France's leading political scientists, he was a Jew who, as a child, fled Germany to escape anti-Semitic persecution, and subsequently played a fundamental role in the

Franco-German rapprochement. On June 19, the "Courrier des lecteurs" column contained nothing but criticism, some of it abusive. The column was organized by the same Éric Conan. The latter had not bothered to inform Alfred Grosser of the publication of carefully selected critical letters. Alfred Grosser, Chairman of the Supervisory Board of *L'Express,* was outraged by this type of procedure and resigned. When it comes to morality and dignity, I'd rather side with Alfred Grosser than Éric Conan.

On December 7, 2001, *Valeurs actuelles* published "L'enquête: pourquoi les Juifs de France ont peur?" (Investigation: why French Jews are afraid). Michel Gurfinkiel, a committed defender of Israel, reported on a year of anti-Semitic violence. A photo illustrating the article showed burnt books after an attack on a synagogue, under the caption: "A situation that some of the media seem to have become accustomed to". This hard-right newspaper blamed the left. According to the article's author, the rise of anti-Semitism, particularly prevalent among the far left and the Greens, "is now affecting the PS itself, long reputed to be pro-Israeli and philosemitic. The Boniface affair was a real bombshell in this respect. On August 4, Pascal Boniface, director of IRIS, an organization close to the PS, published a text in *Le Monde* entitled 'Lettre à un ami israélien' ('Letter to an Israeli friend'). In fact, it's a pro-Palestinian pamphlet. But it is above all its conclusion that attracts attention: by supporting Israel too much, the community runs the risk of isolating itself too much, particularly in the face of the Muslim community... A sort of threat. And for many French Jews, the key to the attacks they have been suffering since the previous October." So I was responsible for anti-Semitic attacks.

In fact, the two weeklies were reprinting a press kit put together by the CRIF on anti-Semitic acts. It had been widely reported in the press, but, citing the source, some journalists pointed out that one could not equate the burning of synagogues with anonymous insults. Let alone attribute the cause to me! *Valeurs actuelles* and *L'Express* not only took up the case themselves, without specifying the source and using all the arguments, but also the language provided orally that concerned me.

Almost simultaneously, the two weekly columns I'd been writing in *La Voix du Nord* and *Nice-Matin*, which up until then had given full satisfaction to the editorial staff, were discontinued. In each case, at the insistence of local Jewish authorities, who were concerned that I should be allowed to express myself after the uproar my article had caused within the "community". Let's imagine for a moment that Muslim associations demand that a column be shut down because its author has taken positions on the Middle East conflict that are not to their liking. This intolerable attack on freedom of expression would have been immediately denounced, and people would have protested against this unacceptable communitarianism. But nothing of the sort.

In *Actualité juive* of September 6, 2002, a page under the heading "anti-Zionism" was devoted to me. The article, entitled "L'affaire Boniface" (The Boniface affair), stated that "the affair" was causing a stir in the Jewish community. I was said to have attacked the Jewish community "violently" through "poisonous insinuations". It was signed Martin Perez, pseudonym of Clément Weill-Raynal. This was to open a new chapter of articles dedicated to me by the same author, in which I was each time accused of violently attacking the Jewish community. He distorted my note, omitting to specify that I had always spoken out in favor of the two-state solution, i.e. the existence of Israel within internationally recognized borders, and that I had always condemned terrorism. This type of article was bound to arouse fear and hostility in readers.

The next day, I received a phone call from Pierre Lellouche, a long-standing member of the IRIS board of directors. Having just discovered the article published in *Le Monde* a year earlier, he explained the sensitivity of the Jewish community and proposed a meeting. The September 11th attacks, which were mobilizing both of us professionally in an intensive way, prevented this contact. Pierre Lellouche subsequently sent Serge Weinberg a letter of resignation. To show his credentials, he must have sent a copy of his letter to *Actualité juive,* which immediately published it, indicating that he had resigned from IRIS. Pierre Lellouche does not have a highly developed communitarian streak, but he did not want to engage in a power struggle.

Between the two rounds of the 2002 presidential election, Christopher Caldwell of the neoconservative *Weekly Standard* asked to meet with me to discuss the links between foreign policy and the electoral debate. Despite his opinions, I agreed to meet him, always ready for debate. Moreover, I find that many American neoconservatives are intellectually better equipped than their French clones. He asks me about my 2001 memo and focuses his questions on anti-Semitism in France. But the conversation is cordial. So I'm all the more surprised when I read his article, soberly entitled "Liberté, égalité, judéophobie", in which he describes a France set on fire by violent Arab youths, evokes the "benladenization" of the suburbs and, in the paragraph devoted to me, dares the term "bonifascism". This neologism will be regularly taken up by the pro-Israeli far right, as well as by Bernard-Henri Lévy (BHL). It implied, of course, that only a fascist could criticize the Israeli government... And that, being one, I was naturally the other.

Hard Times

Created from scratch, IRIS initially had the minimal structure needed to exist as an association: a president, a treasurer and a general secretary. Subsequently, the Board of Directors expanded to include just the "hard core" of the team. Our activities also expanded: in addition to L'Année stratégique, IRIS had created a quarterly journal, organized colloquia, carried out research and studies, and participated in leading the strategic debate. After a few years, I decided to open up the Board of Directors to outside members. Some of us feared being dispossessed of the tool in which we were participating, whereas I was convinced that it was essential to our growth. Pascal Lamy, at the time number 2 at Crédit Lyonnais, with whom I was in contact and whose taste for intellectual debate I knew, accepted the position of Chairman. He was convinced of the need to develop think tanks in France, given how far behind other European countries, not to mention the United States, were in this area. Shortly afterwards, however, he was appointed European Commissioner, a position incompatible with the presidency of IRIS.

So I turned to Marc-Antoine Jamet, Laurent Fabius' chief of staff at the French National Assembly. It was he who suggested I turn to Serge Weinberg, one of his close friends, who headed the Pinault-Printemps-Redoute (PPR) group, now known as Kering. I made an appointment with him, and he readily agreed to take on the presidency of IRIS. A happy and harmonious collaboration was to develop. Serge Weinberg, despite his heavy workload, knew how to make himself available and attentive to my requests. He helped IRIS acquire a new dimension. At the critical moment of the attacks, he behaved impeccably towards me, defending me against accusations of anti-Semitism and staking his reputation on mine. But the burden became too heavy as the attacks intensified.

Within the Board of Directors, the most unexpected, violent and outrageous attack came from the man I'd known the longest: François Heisbourg. In a letter sent to Serge Weinberg, copied to every member of the Board, he accused me of holding the Jews of France accountable for Israel's policies. He had had no prior exchange with me. I had known F. Heisbourg since 1984, when he was a member of Charles Hernu's cabinet and I was in the PS's international sector. I had written a note on the pacifist movement in France, which had caught his attention. We began a fruitful working collaboration and friendly relationship, to the point of publishing a book in 1986[26]

---

26. Pascal Boniface, François Heisbourg, *La puce, les hommes et la bombe*, Hachette, Paris, 1986.

under both our signatures. We always kept in close touch. If I were anti-Semitic, he would have realized it long ago... Serge Weinberg, who had always had a relatively low tolerance of his arrogance, replied very curtly, expressing surprise at the "unworthy procedure of accusing me of anti-Semitism" and considering that his approach was part of a general negative attitude towards IRIS.

A board meeting was held in spring 2002, to discuss freedom of expression and its limits. We had a frank and transparent dialogue. Some members, while supporting me, explained that, as director, I should adopt a "smoother" expression and avoid polemics. (Regrettable as it may be in contemporary French society, some subjects are more inflammatory than others). I replied that I hadn't chosen this profession to curb my freedom, and that the raison d'être of IRIS was precisely to allow total freedom of expression in accordance with the laws of the Republic.

In 2002, on the first anniversary of the September 11th attacks, I was interviewed at length in the Swiss newspaper *Le Temps*, in particular on the notion of the "axis of evil" developed by George W. Bush in his State of the Union address in January. I explained why I found this concept, which was to "justify" the Iraq war, as questionable as the "rogue states" concept developed earlier. Indeed, these concepts seemed to me to be of variable geometry, putting forward "moral" criteria only against countries that opposed the United States. If it was a question of denouncing the lack of democracy or nuclear research, the list of countries concerned was much broader than that of the countries targeted by the American president, and some—like Pakistan and Saudi Arabia—were among the best allies of the United States. I added, somewhat ironically, that there was one country with nuclear weapons, where the generals wielded a great deal of power without the United States being concerned: Israel. I was immediately accused of calling Israel part of the axis of evil, when in fact I was saying that there was no such axis, and making a mockery of it by using Israel as an example. But humor and pro-Israeli ultras don't mix. This was another good way of distorting my words in an attempt to silence me.

On November 7, 2002, a Board of Directors meeting was convened at IRIS. Agenda: "IRIS governance". The IRIS Director is appointed by the Board, but does not sit on it. He nevertheless attends its meetings and prepares them with the Chairman. This time, however, there was no contact with Serge Weinberg. In fact, everyone understood the purpose of the meeting: my dismissal. Serge Weinberg, who had supported me from the start, was giving up. The board meeting took place in a particularly charged atmosphere. Shortly before, one of the members, Patrick Careil, had sent a letter calling for my dismissal. I wondered what was the best course of action, since this climate had affected me so much over the past year, and I was really getting tired of it. I felt it was unfair to be ousted from the institute I had created from scratch, on the basis of unfounded accusations. I also found it unacceptable that, in a democratic state, freedom of expression should be flouted to such an extent. But, concerned about the survival of IRIS and the fate of its employees, I was ready to throw in the towel, even though

I was deeply worried about my professional future. Four close colleagues and friends, Didier Billion, Jean-Pierre Maulny, Alexandre Tuaillon and Boris Contesse, whose professional and friendly support had never failed me, informed me that they too would leave if the Board decided to oust me. It was a choice that was both supportive and significant: a refusal to work for an institute that had undergone a change of management on these grounds. Their solidarity moved me and convinced me that IRIS could be dismantled, even if I left its management, and that its survival depended on it. Serge Weinberg explained that it had become impossible to continue as I was, that my statements were endangering the institution and that it was impossible for me to work on developing it in the face of the hostility I was arousing. The majority of board members felt that, although the situation was delicate, it required us not to give in to threats to freedom of expression from community organizations[27]. On the Board of Directors, Philippe Seguin and Jean Musitelli were particularly aggressive. They asked Serge Weinberg whether pressure from the CRIF justified his change of attitude. Roger Cukierman, then President of the CRIF, had written to the Ministers of Defense and Foreign Affairs asking them to end their relations, including, and above all, their contractual and financial relations with IRIS. Serge Weinberg replied that he had nothing to do with CRIF's demands and reactions.

---

27. It was not yet fashionable to condemn communitarianism, but this was clearly a case where it constituted a clear-cut threat to freedom.

It's true that, in the face of pressure, potential private partners turned away, and that the controversy, skilfully fuelled, kept many potential cooperations at bay. But, in reality, the person who seems to have tipped the balance was Bernard-Henri Lévy (BHL), who had friendly ties with Serge Weinberg. At the very start of the controversy, Serge Weinberg explained to me that, after speaking to several of his Jewish community contacts, he had noticed a generational phenomenon: the older generation had been painfully aware of my note, while the younger ones were not particularly offended by it. He gave me the example of BHL, who saw nothing scandalous in it. So he changed his mind for reasons I still don't understand... He even decided to have my head. BHL was also very close to François Pinault, and Serge Weinberg was director of the PPR group, owned by Pinault. I left the room to make way for the vote, which rejected my dismissal. I was nevertheless particularly stunned. Serge Weinberg resigned from the Board along with a small third of the other members.

Serge Weinberg's resignation was, of course, a blow. On a personal level, even if I felt a little bitter about the way our collaboration had ended, I still had immense respect for him. I understood his reasons. IRIS was 1% of his time and responsibilities, 99% of his worries. Chairing the Board was a service rendered: he had nothing to gain, found himself at the heart of a maelstrom and taking blows from all sides. His professional position was even in jeopardy. He had courageously defended me during his presidency, and I had been impressed by his intellectual and human qualities. For IRIS, the blow was even harder. His resignation led to the resignation of other members who had come at his request, such as Baudouin Prot, director of the BNP Paribas group, and Nicolas Sarkozy, whom Serge Weinberg had brought on board. However, Sarkozy had shortly before indicated that he was not required to take a position on what I had said[28]. Laurent Fabius, undoubtedly to avoid taking the brunt of the blow, remained silent until the end of his term[29].

Thanks to Serge Weinberg's contacts, contacts and projects multiplied. Although it didn't reach the advertising pagination of *Politique internationale*, IRIS began to receive advertising, which enabled it to be partially financed. On the strength of his name or recommendations, Serge Weinberg opened many doors, giving IRIS not only visibility, but also a different dimension to that previously achieved. Funding prospects were no longer the same. All this came to an abrupt halt, and not only was the development in sight stopped dead in its tracks, but we had to fight against those who wanted to drain existing resources. If it hadn't been for this affair, IRIS would certainly be a much different organization today. That's the way it is, and there's no need to regret it. If nothing else, the difficulties had the merit of spurring innovation.

Arthur Paecht, who in 2002 had not sought renewal of his mandate as a UDF (Union pour la démocratie française) deputy, accepted the difficult task of succeeding him in these

---

28. See Appendix 2.

29. Some of my "friends" circulated the "news" that he had condemned my comments. He didn't. He personally presented me with the insignia of Officer of the Legion of Honor in 2013, and in 2015 came to deliver a lecture to IRIS students despite an overloaded schedule.

more than uncertain times. I had known him since 1986, when I worked at the French National Assembly, and had always appreciated his great independence and integrity. It so happened that, of Austrian origin, both his Jewish parents had been killed by the Nazis, but had taken the precaution of sending their son into hiding in France. He could hardly be accused of being insensitive to anti-Semitism. In fact, he made the same remark to Roger Cukierman when the latter asked him to resign as President of IRIS. In 2005, Arthur Paecht was forced to put his Parisian activities on hold in order to remain close to his ailing wife. Jacques Boyon, to whom I would also like to pay tribute, succeeded him.

François Thual, who was a personal friend and one of the first to join IRIS after its creation, was a civil servant in the Ministry of Defense, seconded to the President of the Senate and parliamentary advisor on international issues for the Union Centrist group. This enabled IRIS to organize colloquia in the prestigious setting of the Senate, which was of considerable interest to a fledgling research center with such limited resources. As for François Thual, he found in IRIS the opportunity to express himself publicly and even to publish, which was impossible for him within his professional framework. We often had long discussions together on geopolitical issues, in which there was little disagreement, including on the Middle East. He had become deputy director of IRIS in the spring of 2002, after my note and the polemic launched against me. But when the latter flared up after the publication of Est-il permis de critiquer Israël, he changed his attitude. Was he afraid of the professional consequences?

Was he afraid of seeing his comfortable position in the Union Centrist group called into question? In any case, he resigned as deputy director of IRIS, citing disagreements he had never expressed before. I understood that he had been "worked over" by Frédéric Encel, with whom he had Masonic links. Indeed, his resignation was interpreted by the extreme right-wing pro-Israeli websites[30] and by Encel himself, in a letter he widely circulated, as the beginning of the demise of IRIS. Entitled "La maison vide de l'IRIS" ("The empty house of IRIS"), his letter took stock of the defections, announcing that IRIS would not survive. It was certainly Frédéric Encel's undermining that led to François Thual's resignation. Nevertheless, shortly afterwards, they began to work together, publishing the book Géopolitique d'Israël, the content of which was unlikely to arouse the wrath of the European Union[31].

I was no longer just the man to kill. IRIS also had to be killed. Hence the pressure on board members, ministries and companies working with us. Some gave in, others resisted. IRIS almost disappeared at that point.

---

30. F. Thual had to send a denial to *Actualité juive,* which, in issue no. 806, had presented his resignation in a way that did little to reflect reality, again under the fiendish pen of Clément Weill-Raynal.

31. During my first contact with Frédéric Encel—a debate on France Culture about my book *Est-il permis de critiquer Israël?*—he claimed not to be Jewish. In addition to the immense propensity for lying and dissimulation he was already demonstrating, this assertion was supposed to strengthen his case. Support for the theses of the Israeli government (since that's what it was all about) carried more weight if it came from a non-Jew. Yet the same man had repeatedly attacked "people who have Jewish-sounding names and who write articles in which they promote *self-hatred*".

A Time of Red Roses

The day after the first round of the 2002 presidential election, an editorial published on the Consistoire de Paris website[32] offered an explanation for the defeat of Lionel Jospin and the presence of Jean-Marie Le Pen in the second round. Jean-François Strouf wrote, under the title "Chronicle of an unheralded cataclysm": "Let's not exonerate from their responsibilities the unconscious politicians who made Le Pen's bed in France, and there are more of them than we think. As French citizens, as Jews and as friends of Israel, we are triply concerned. When Pascal Boniface calls on the Socialist Party to distance itself from Israel, to marginalize France's Jewish community so as not to alienate the Beur vote, he is essentially saying that the caricatured Third Worldism of the Quai d'Orsay, the Greens and the far left will necessarily be accompanied by a lack of empathy for

---

32. www.consistoire.org

the victims of anti-Semitic attacks in France. Since October 2000, demonstrations orchestrated by the FIDH, MRAP, trade unions and parties of the left and far left have featured the booing of Israel at the head of the procession and shouts of 'Death to the Jews' at the tail end, followed by anti-Semitic attacks on synagogues, Jewish schools, school buses, teenagers playing sport, identifiable passers-by, etc. This is where the few hundred anti-Semitic acts of aggression have gone. This is where the few hundred thousand votes Lionel Jospin missed to give France the democratic second round to which the vast majority of French people aspired have gone."

Laurent Azoulay, one of the heads of the Val-de-Marne PS federation, sent a circular letter[33] shedding light on Jospin's surprise defeat in the first round: I was responsible! I had been guilty of publishing articles in the media, but also, as the ultimate provocation, "in the press of the Jewish community". No need to point out to Mr. Azoulay that I had merely used a legal right of reply... He continued: "One hundred and ninety thousand votes were needed for Lionel Jospin to reach the second round, including that of a large part of the Jewish community, which massively supported Alain Madelin... one of the few candidates to take a clear and courageous stance on the Middle East conflict... The Jewish vote doesn't exist... except when provoked."

Laurent Azoulay quietly asserted the existence of a Jewish vote, indexed to the attitude of political leaders towards the Middle East conflict. To hold me responsible for Jospin's

---

33. Entitled "Le Pen has Pascal Boniface to thank"...

defeat in 2002 was, moreover, to attribute to me a dispropor-
tionate importance, in view of the many factors that explained
this surprise defeat[34]. In any case, it was amusing to see that
those who had criticized me for evoking a community vote,
and who kept repeating that there was no such thing as a
Jewish vote, were now attributing their champion's defeat
to the Jewish vote. Indeed, those within the Socialist Party
who criticized Lionel Jospin for being "lukewarm" in his
fight against anti-Semitism and for showing insufficient
solidarity with Israel, while repeating anxiety-inducing
rhetoric aimed at French Jews, may well have contributed
to alienating some of his voters. PS communitarians played
their part in Jospin's defeat. It is also likely that, in line with
the warning, the feeling of a "double standard" against the
Palestinians alienated some voters, particularly among
young people, and not just Arabs. In fact, Lionel Jospin lost
on both counts. His distancing himself from Israel had not
been noted by supporters of the Palestinian cause. So it
didn't do him any good with them. On the other hand, it was
very much noticed by pro-Israeli ultras, including socialists,
and therefore did him a disservice in their eyes. For many,
the two images that remained were Jacques Chirac's spat
with Israeli soldiers in Jerusalem in 1996 and Lionel Jospin's
stoning on the campus of Bir Zeit University in 2000. In
February, during the latter's trip to Israel, Pierre Moscovici

34. Multiple candidacies on the left, voting during school vacations,
demobilization due to overconfidence in a victory that was supposed to
be a foregone conclusion, confusion between the first and second round
campaigns, and so on.

told journalists Éric Aeschimann and Christophe Boltanski: "The Jewish vote counts", in reference to the spring 2001 municipal elections in which Paris, with its large Jewish community, was a key issue[35]. In fact, the question of the existence of the Jewish vote is of little importance as long as most politicians are convinced of its reality. Their perception leads to its creation.

Dominique Strauss-Kahn (DSK), who had said of José Bové, who had just been expelled from Ramallah by the Israelis, that he didn't know what to invent to get in front of the cameras, had, for his part, added fuel to the fire.

Pro-Israel ultras, members of the PS, set up the Cercle Léon Blum at this time, under the leadership of Laurent Azoulay, who also had business dealings with Israel. The official aim was to combat anti-Semitism and, more specifically, "left-wing anti-Semitism". In fact, it was a circle set up above all to combat the threat I represented. The aim was for the PS not to abandon its pro-Israeli stance, whatever the government, or at least not to become critical of Israel by blaming it for the continuation of the conflict and criticizing the occupation and the repression that ensued. It would have been more logical and coherent to call this circle Guy Mollet but, of course, that was less salesy. Léon Blum is a mythical figure of the Left, who also suffered anti-Semitic attacks. But it soon became clear that this new organization would have difficulty getting beyond the small circle of pro-Israeli ultras within the PS. They managed to recruit a few more people,

---

35. Alain Gresh, *Un chant d'amour*, La Découverte, Paris, 2017, p. 152.

some out of conviction or lack of global perspective (it's hard not to be against anti-Semitism), others out of cynicism (this current is too powerful within the party for me to find any interest in opposing it).

The Cercle Léon Blum did not mention any form of racism other than anti-Semitism, the latter objective being itself biased. The Cercle was not going to come to the defense of all Jews under attack. When Jews were specifically attacked for opposing Ariel Sharon, there was no reaction. A far-right website had placed yellow stars in front of the names of French Jews critical of Israel's government, and the Cercle Léon Blum had not reacted. Yet it was as Jews that they were attacked. Rony Brauman was described as a "Jewish traitor". Esther Benbassa, Dominique Vidal, Alain Gresh, Stéphane Hessel, Edgar Morin, Charles Enderlin, were infamously attacked as Jews for criticizing the Israeli government. Eyal Sivan received a letter containing a bullet from a revolver with the words: "The next one won't arrive in the mail" without any reaction from this circle, which sometimes even participated in it. On the other hand, any criticism of Sharon as a great man of the left, as Rony Brauman, Eyal Sivan and Esther Benbassa had dared to do, was immediately equated with anti-Semitism. Behind the rhetoric (the fight against anti-Semitism), the real intention was to give sanctuary to the Israeli government. In a letter of invitation to a colloquium the Cercle was organizing on November 25, 2003, its president, Laurent Azoulay, set the tone: "We need to win back an electorate that left us in 2002." And I was the one accused of electioneering...

In 2001, Pierre Schapira, a long-standing friend, became deputy for international relations at Paris City Hall. He was also in charge of Israel in the PS's international sector. But my note had created more than a chill between us, and he had forbidden any contact between his departments and IRIS, even though we were proposing training courses, symposia and expertise. He even went so far as to perform what might be considered a particularly humorous gesture: putting his hand to his throat when Romain Levy, his deputy, who was also a former student of mine, expressed regret that the town hall was refusing proposals from IRIS, boycotted by the international delegation even though we were organizing dozens of events, free of charge and open to the public.

Élisabeth Schemla, a former journalist with *L'Express* and *Le Nouvel Observateur*, had just set up the website Proche-Orient.info with considerable resources, with the aim of "re-establishing objective information on the Middle East". Many thought it was more a question of having a media offering a positive image of Israel, at a time when this was deteriorating, and to strike a blow against those who criticized its government. Elisabeth Schemla has a temperament that can best be described as volcanic. Immediately after my interview with Le *Temps, in which* I was presented as the inspirer of the French Left and Lionel Jospin's advisor, she accused me of equating Israel with Middle Eastern dictatorships and placing it on the axis of evil. It was a singular misrepresentation of what I'd said, and one that was to spark off another intense campaign against me. A few Socialists, staunch supporters of Israel's defense, began circulating a petition calling for my expulsion from the Socialist Party. Of course, none of them had bothered to contact me for a debate. It was a Jewish friend of mine, a member of the PS, who was contacted to sign the petition, who warned me about it. I imagine that the promoters of this petition are all up in arms against the campaigns to boycott Israel, and that they are all very "Charlie". One can only be dubious about the behavior of individuals who claim freedom of debate on condition that their opponents are not allowed to express themselves... I imagine that many of them are not even aware of this immense contradiction.

The leaders of the CRIF went on the attack, demanding my exclusion from the PS or, failing that, the revocation of my title of delegate for strategic affairs. François Hollande and Henri Nallet stood firm, both refusing. The PS leadership found itself divided between those who wanted my head, those who shared my views, those who found the reaction of the former excessive and others who felt it was best not to confront them. I received support from all sides. To send a message to my detractors, Alain Richard, Minister of Defense, personally awarded me the insignia of Chevalier de la Légion d'Honneur in December 2001. Lionel Jospin invited me to accompany him on an official trip to Moscow in February 2002. Hubert Védrine's public support never failed me. Finally, Claude Bartolone, then Minister for Urban Affairs, invited me for a tête-à-tête lunch. Bariza and Saad Khiari, along with Fayçal Douhane and Ouarda Karrai, found these attacks unbearable, and came to my rescue, forging a true friendship that unites us to this day.

After the PS congress in Dijon, the organization chart of the international secretariat was slow to be made public. Several weeks went by without it being published, leaving the microcosm in a state of expectation. In the end, it became clear that my presence within the secretariat was the problem. While I enjoyed the support of a very large number of people, probably more numerous than those who wanted me dead, the latter were far more determined. Pierre Moscovici, who had succeeded Henri Nallet as International Secretary, invited me to lunch in June. I'd known him before he became Minister and had a cordial relationship with him. He wasn't part of the circle of pro-Israeli ultras, but having declared that "the Jewish vote exists", he acted coolly, taking into account the balance of power. He was also very close to DSK. He must have been wondering what would cause him the least trouble and, obviously, firing me was the best option. Over lunch, he told me how horrified he was by the colonization of the Occupied Territories, how little he liked the Israeli right, and so on. But in France, we had to calm things down, because the subject was unleashing passions, and perhaps it would be better, if only temporarily, if I left the post of Delegate for Strategic Affairs. I had no problem with that. I had accepted the title without asking for it, and I had no electoral ambitions. So I wasn't looking to move up the ranks of the PS. In fact, it rather hindered my freedom of expression. I realized that if I'd produced exactly the same article without being a member of the PS, I'd never have stirred up such a storm. So I let her know that I accepted the decision. On the other hand, I wanted it to be the fruit

The Anti-Semite

of mutual agreement and not to appear as a sanction, as this would have taken a different political turn. Pierre Moscovici was quite open to the idea, and we discussed the possibility of my being invited in a visible way and given prominence at the next PS summer university. We parted as good friends, talking about the forthcoming Euro soccer tournament, both of us being fans of the game. But on June 22, a major meeting organized by community bodies took place: "12 heures pour l'amitié France-Israël" (12 hours for France-Israel friendship). Meyer Habib, who chaired the organizing committee, denounced French foreign policy. Nothing very new under the sun. Netanyahu honored the meeting with his presence, and Hollande took a turn, accompanied by DSK. There was talk of the rift between the Left and the Jews, while Alain Madelin and Nicolas Sarkozy were warmly welcomed.

In *Le Monde* on June 24, we read: "But it was the former Finance Minister, Dominique Strauss-Kahn, who most vigorously tried to pick up the pieces with a Jewish community visibly angry with the left: 'As a Jew, I have a natural sympathy for Israel. As a socialist, I have political sympathy. The Left has let you down. There were unauthorized notes [alluding to a text written by academic Pascal Boniface advocating a change in the Socialist Party's policy towards Israel]. They were miserable". And Mr. Strauss-Kahn concluded: "I can tell you that the left is back".

It was more than I could bear. Indulging in vindictiveness in front of a white-hot crowd in the presence of that great man of the left, Benyamin Netanyahu... If that wasn't communitarianism of the lowest order, how could I define it? The term "miserable" was infamous, and above all the concept of "unauthorized notes" was beyond comprehension. Do you have to ask permission to write a note? How could a former academic like DSK utter such an enormity? Everyone has the right to write notes, just as everyone has the right to read them, throw them in the garbage can, think about them or ignore them. So I informed François Hollande of my decision to leave the PS. In my letter of resignation, dated July 2, 2003, I accused Israel's friends of demonizing me and deplored the fact that priority was given to those with an "ethnic vision of the conflict" and "the return in force of communitarianism". I also denounced the pro-Israeli ultras "who have created a real fear among many French Jews, which they have used to justify the need to oust me".

"If you need permission to write notes, I have no business in this party. I'd rather take back my freedom. In any case, the debate of ideas doesn't go through the PS. Many people in the party agree with me, but discussion is impossible. It's a real taboo."

He replied that, knowing me, he was not surprised by the frankness and sincerity of my letter. But he could not accept either the introduction or the demonstration...

I also wrote to DSK, whom I had known since my days as assistant to the Socialist group at the National Assembly, where he had been elected deputy in 1986. I reminded him of our good working relationship, in which I had always taken great pleasure, because of his intellectual abilities, his cordiality and the immediate closeness he knew how to create. I reminded him that, a few months earlier, he had come to Berlin to take part in a Franco-German circle co-organized by IRIS, to discuss the Middle East with me. We didn't see eye to eye, but it was an intellectual debate, with no prejudices. I concluded with the astonishing concept of "unauthorized notes", writing that what was miserable didn't seem to be my note, but the way I was treated: accusations of anti-Semitism, distortions of my remarks to disqualify them, accusations of communitarianism, not to mention numerous personal and professional threats. By stigmatizing me in front of a crowd that included a few "excitements", I felt he had added fuel to the fire.

I received many messages of solidarity, including from Manuel Valls who, at the time, had not opted for the ultra-pro-Israeli line he now takes[36]. Pierre Moscovici explained his position in a letter sent to an activist protesting my departure[37].

I've kept many contacts in the PS, and even friends, but this episode showed how difficult it is for a political party to open up to intellectuals who wish to maintain a freedom of expression that can clash with the constraints inherent in partisan life. Both Manuel Valls and François Hollande were members of the IRIS board of directors[38]. The board was made up of personalities from all the main political parties, who felt it would be useful for a research center on strategic issues to work in complete freedom, without yielding to the

---

36. See Appendix 4.
37. See Appendix 3.
38. From 2007 to 2010 for the former and from 1998 to 2007 for the latter.

various pressure groups. On numerous occasions, the CRIF has expressed concern to its leaders about my possible return to the PS structure, including in 2012. Rest assured, I will never again join a political party.

In 2011, at the Summer University of the French Socialist Party (PS), I bumped into Patrick Klugman, who asked me about my book Les intellectuels faussaires[39], telling me that he'd given up trying to sue me for libel for what I'd written in the chapter on BHL. I replied that this was regrettable, as it promised to be an amusing trial. A former leader of the UEJF, Patrick Klugman is a left-wing figure in Judaism who, on several occasions, has openly mentioned his ambition to become president of the CRIF. As a lawyer, he's not quite available to take on the full-time job of deputy mayor of Paris in charge of international relations and the French-speaking world, but he has enough time for what really matters: relations with Israel.

In 2013, meeting David Kessler, I suggested that he bring together a small group of fifteen to twenty people, considered pro-Israeli and pro-Palestinian, although I find these categories artificial and reductive, committed to the two-state solution. He replied that it wasn't really up to him, but that the idea was interesting and that I should talk to Klugman about it. I contacted Klugman. I explained to him that, in my mind, the idea was to organize a non-public meeting, possibly to be followed by others, whose purpose

---

39. Pascal BONIFACE, *Les intellectuels faussaires. Le triomphe médiatique des experts en mensonge*, Jean-Claude Gawsewitch éditeur, Paris, 2011.

was simply to set the framework for the debate and limit the negative effects of importing the Middle East conflict into France. It was never followed up. The question of the Israeli-Palestinian conflict continued to be the blind spot in the PS's vision.

In July 2015, Omar Sy was interviewed by the Israeli channel i24NEWS. France's favorite actor shared his views on a wide range of social issues, but when asked about the Israeli-Palestinian conflict, he replied that he "didn't have enough information". I ironically tweeted that, if he didn't have all the information, he at least had "a sense of balance of power". I was immediately accused of reinventing the Protocols of the Elders of Zion and implying that the Jews controlled the cinema. Of course, I hadn't said or suggested anything of the sort, but I was making the simple observation that even (and especially?) very popular personalities are afraid to speak out on the Middle East conflict for fear of taking a beating. At least, speaking out in favor of the Palestinians, as no artist who has expressed solidarity with Israel has ever suffered the slightest backlash. On the other hand, taking a stand in favor of Palestinian rights is immediately presented as aggression towards Israel, not to say proof of anti-Semitism, which leads to widespread silence. It would have been difficult for Omar Sy to write an ode to Israeli democracy, which a large part of his audience would not have understood, so he cautiously preferred to ignore it. No more, no less. Artistic circles, which can easily take a stand on many social and even international issues (Tibet, etc.), avoid the one that arouses the most passion.

They simply don't want to find themselves in the middle of violent polemics[40].

Patrick Klugman tweeted angrily:

If anything was "unveiled" on this occasion, it was Klugman's communitarianism—though in fact already largely established—rather than my conspiracy. For, of course, Klugman believes he is the arbiter of situations and has the right to hand out the cards.

In a tweet, I pointed out to Patrick Klugman that his selection criterion for managing his delegation was the absence of criticism of Benyamin Netanyahu. He lashed out with numerous tweets in which he wrote, among

---

40. There are some rare exceptions to this pusillanimity on the part of French artists: in 2013, Mélissa Theuriau did a report for UNICEF in Gaza, showing the difficulties Palestinian children face in their daily lives; François Cluzet questioned Jean-François Copé on the 1 p.m. news on France 2 on November 8, 2009, about France's inaction in securing the release of Salah Hamouri.

other niceties, that I was "not a friend of Palestine" but "an obsessive anti-Israeli". He compared me to Dieudonné, accused me of being financed by Qatar... In short, he repeated the traditional accusations levelled at me by the pro-Israeli far right, and ended up calling me an imbecile. Can you imagine any other elected official insulting a citizen in this way without provoking a reaction? Klugman rightly felt a strong sense of impunity. No one at City Hall admonished him, apart from Ian Brossat, a Communist councillor from the 20th arrondissement, who lent me his support. This proves, if proof were needed, that the dividing line on this issue is not between Jews and non-Jews, but between universalist Jews like Ian Brossat and communitarianist Jews like Patrick Klugman.

Can you imagine an international relations deputy committed to the cause of Palestine, refusing all contact to people who are insufficiently devoted to it? He'd find it hard to stay in his job, and if he were to insult one of his fellow-citizens for these reasons, he'd be in trouble too, including in court.

In view of our exchanges on social networks, Nathalie Coste, a friend who teaches at the Lycée Saint-Exupéry in Mantes-la-Jolie, sent him the following letter:

"To Patrick Klugman, Deputy Mayor of Paris

"I've been silently reading your Twitter exchanges with Pascal Boniface. Beyond the brutal and rude tone, which shocks the elected representative and teacher that I am, I am particularly outraged by the insinuations and/or accusations of anti-Semitism made against him.

Indeed, I know Pascal Boniface well, who has been working with us on a voluntary basis for the past eight years at the Lycée Saint-Exupéry in Mantes-la-Jolie, supporting candidates from our school in their preparation for the Sciences Po entrance exam under the 'priority education agreements.'

"In addition to his sincere support and constant presence without media coverage, his invaluable scientific input and the many contributions of IRIS conferences, Pascal Boniface comes to our school three times a year to meet our students and answer their questions on the geopolitics of today's world, as well as on French society.

"Some sometimes confused teenagers have, for a minority of them, a totally biased and partial view of the Israeli-Palestinian conflict and a solely religious reading of Middle Eastern troubles. On numerous occasions, I can attest to the great determination and conviction shown by Pascal Boniface in these exchanges, forcefully condemning any anti-Semitic slip and patiently reverting to a rational and historical discourse in support of those we develop in our courses.

"More than that, in fact, as few intellectuals do, he accepts to 'confront' these inaudible and disturbing discourses in order to better fight them, because they must be fought!

"We, practitioners in the field, know that we can win the day in these debates on these subjects, not by ranting and raving through the media, but by rolling up our sleeves and coming to meet those who are just teenagers in the making, sometimes in a strong quest for identity, and who need intellectual rigor IN dialogue, from credible and sincere adults who don't scorn them or peremptorily install them in the role of the anti-Semitic suburban savage.

"I've seen Pascal Boniface forcefully convey this message to teenagers, urging them not to fall into the unhealthy traps of anti-Semitism, conspiracy and radicalism, and inviting them to think and learn about everything.

"He is, along with other intellectuals who are willing to come to our suburban school without fuss, where not everything is going so badly, and where yes, the Shoah, the Algerian war and Middle Eastern conflicts are normally taught, a precious partner far removed from the image you give of him.

"I would like to thank you for giving credence to my words, which are guided by sincerity and not by any spirit of media polemics, which I am far removed from, just a few days before I return to my students.

"Yours sincerely, Mr. Klugman, in wishing you a warm welcome, please accept the expression of my profound republican and humanist sentiments."

She never got an answer. Is Patrick Klugman embarrassed by the substance of the question? Or did he feel that his rank exempted him from answering to a simple suburban teacher? Probably a bit of both.

I wasn't invited to the 2015 PS summer university in La Rochelle. But I was an important topic of conversation. At one table, Jérôme Guedj and David Assouline (PS deputy and senator), Frédéric Haziza (journalist at LCP—AN and Radio J), and a few others, were expressing all the bad things they had to think about me, loud enough for the neighbors to hear. David Assouline sharply reproached the boss of Beur FM for inviting me on Abdelkrim Branine's show to talk about my book Les pompiers pyromanes. Nacer Kettane, listening only to his courage, which told him nothing, murmured soft explanations[41]. He later explained that he did not wish to quarrel with David Assouline, whose influence he feared. It is curious, to say the least, that a member of parliament, who no doubt proclaimed himself to be "Charlie", should reproach a radio station owner for inviting me...

In an exchange with David Assouline, he blamed me for fuelling anti-Semitism "since 2001 at least", through "my obsession with trying to induce that anti-Israeli speech would be gagged by the lobby or dominant decision-makers". Admirable logic, which amounts to asking me not to complain about the attacks to which I am subjected by pro-Israeli lobbies, so as not to fuel anti-Semitism. Perhaps it would have been better not to silence me for daring to criticize the Israeli government... In fact, perhaps unconsciously, David Assouline and his friends are developing the same mentality as certain Israeli soldiers based at a checkpoint: do what they want, even if it means making your life miserable, without you complaining, at the risk of making your situation worse...

Ouarda Karrai, an activist who witnessed the scene, criticizes David Assouline for his intolerance. She was astonished that Caroline Fourest had been invited to a

----

41. The geopolitical debate program I was to have hosted on the station in September never saw the light of day.

round-table discussion at the summer university[42] without any opponents. David Assouline retorts: "Do you want her to end up with a bullet in the head? Ouarda Karrai retorts that, beyond wanting to banish me from the media, he didn't react when I was attacked or threatened with death. David Assouline's immediate response: "Serves him right."

The vivacity of communitarianism within the PS seems inexhaustible.

42. Caroline Fourest is the muse of the PS pro-Israeli clan. She does not speak out directly on the Israeli-Palestinian conflict, but her particularly distorted vision of secularism leads her to attack in particular those who would like to assert an autonomous Muslim identity. And she regularly attacks with violence those who are critical of Israel, likening them to "Islamist idiots".

They Voted

The risk for a democracy is to make its foreign policy choices dependent on domestic political considerations, usually electoral. This can result in costly gestures for nations, but useful ones for those in power, seeking to please rather than to be effective. This reasoning is based on a questionable presupposition: that public opinion is incapable of determining long-term issues for itself, and systematically favors the short term.

In my note, I suggested that France's policy in the Middle East should not be based on the weight of different communities, but on universal principles, as France generally claims. As mentioned earlier, one of the arguments put forward, particularly by the PS, to avoid being too critical of Israel, was precisely electoral. It was based on the assumption that French Jews would vote for the candidate or party most friendly to Israel. However, French policy towards the Middle East conflict has not always been subject to the prism of its domestic politics.

In 1967, after the Six-Day War, General de Gaulle abruptly put an end to the Franco-Israeli strategic alliance, one of the major axes of the Fourth Republic's diplomacy. France was Israel's leading supplier of military equipment, and had helped it obtain nuclear weapons. The two countries had joined forces with Great Britain in the disastrous Suez intervention of 1956. In May 1967, before the outbreak of war, de Gaulle declared: "If Israel is attacked, we will not let it be destroyed, but if you attack, we will condemn your initiative."

He predicted an Israeli military victory, but, from the international point of view, "growing difficulties". Regretting that he had not been heard, he added at a press conference in November 1967: "Now [Israel] is organizing an occupation on the territories it has taken, which cannot go on without aggression, repression and expulsion, and where a resistance is manifesting itself which it in turn calls terrorist."

De Gaulle had made a profound break with French policy, against the opinion of the majority of the French population, who were very pro-Israeli at the time. According to an IFOP poll conducted on June 5 and 6, 1967, 58% of French people were sympathetic to Israel (compared with 8% for Arab countries). Of course, the President didn't care about the reactions of the CRIF or other community associations, about a possible Jewish vote, or even about the dominant currents in the French media and society. He had acted as a statesman.

The press was just as favorable to Israel. France-soir even attributed the outbreak of war to Egypt, against all truth, before correcting[43]. Children's literature had its own verse: "But the Arabs aren't happy. They're attacking villages and farms. They want little David to leave. They're not very brave, but they're mean[44]", explains the book *Le Petit David ou Israël raconté aux enfants*, published in 1969. During the 1973 Yom Kippur War, Michel Jobert, the French Minister of Foreign Affairs, wrote: "Does trying to return home constitute unforeseen aggression?"

In March 1982, François Mitterrand, who had condemned the breakdown of the Franco-Israeli alliance in 1967, declared before the Knesset (the Israeli parliament) that the Palestinians must pursue their rights to the end, "which may, when the time comes, mean a state". The speech was made before the war in Lebanon the following summer, which did much to damage Israel's image in France. François Mitterrand went on to rescue Yasser Arafat, who had been surrounded in Beirut in 1982, going against French opinion and, even more so, the generally pro-Israeli Socialist Party. In 1988, he received Arafat in Paris, who declared the charter of the Palestine Liberation Organization (PLO) null and void. The CRIF protested strongly against the visit of the man it considered a terrorist, to which François Mitterrand replied that he intended to "conduct the politics of France, not those of a community". On May 11 1988, receiving representatives

---

43. Dominique VIDAL, "Même de Gaulle était isolé", *Le Monde diplomatique*, June 2007 (https://www.monde-diplomatique.fr/2007/06/BERG/14839).
44. Quoted *in* Alain GRESH, Hélène ALDEGUER, *Un chant d'amour : Israël-Palestine, une histoire française*, La Découverte, Paris, 2017, p. 71.

of the CRIF, he declared: "You have come to see me as French citizens. Well, Jews will vote as they wish. I've seen that there's been a reaction against me and my policies. You'll do as you please. Let me tell you that it doesn't matter, France is something else. It includes many parties other than the Jewish community[45]."

When Prime Minister Jacques Chirac was due to attend the CRIF dinner, he received the speech that the organization's president intended to deliver. The speech contained passages highly critical of French diplomacy in relation to the Israeli-Palestinian conflict. Jacques Chirac protested and threatened not to attend the dinner. The CRIF president agreed to modify his remarks to make them less abrasive.

During the 2012 election campaign, François Hollande pledged to recognize Palestine. The CRIF led a battle against him and in favor of Nicolas Sarkozy. The latter was nevertheless defeated. But in his first speech to the ambassadors in August 2012, François Hollande corrected the text prepared by Paul-Jean Ortiz, his diplomatic adviser, with his own hand, for a formula more in keeping with Nicolas Sarkozy's words of previous years.

In February 2017, François Hollande attended the CRIF dinner as he does every year, where, since Nicolas Sarkozy, the President has given a speech instead of the Prime Minister[46]. Foreign Minister Jean-Marc Ayrault was not invited,

---

45. Quoted *in* Pierre PÉAN, *Dernières volontés, derniers combats, dernières souffrances*, Plon, Paris, 2002.

46. Who accompanies the President to this dinner, along with almost all the ministers.

"punished" for having organized the Middle East peace conference in Paris on January 15, 2017. At the Élysée Palace, as in the government, this caused no stir. François Hollande did not keep his election promise to recognize the State of Palestine. One might have thought that, since the path of negotiation had been pushed to the limit in vain, the French president, who was not standing for re-election, would keep his promise to (re)align himself with the foreign policy of the Fifth Republic and speak out on behalf of France in favor of the right of peoples to self-determination and international law. Not so! On reading his speech, it becomes clear that, in order to please his audience, the President repeats the host's arguments. No journalist has ever bothered to ask François Hollande about the reasons for his change of heart. It can only be explained by the fear of seeing a campaign launched against him and France for anti-Semitism.

François Hollande had, however, been elected against the official community bodies, proving that you can win the presidential election despite their hostility. Emmanuel Macron, elected to the French presidency in May 2017, referred to Gaullo-Mitterrandism on numerous occasions during the election campaign. But he announced that he would not recognize Palestine (at least he doesn't have to betray a commitment afterwards) and spoke out against the Boycott Divestment Sanctions (BDS) movement, which advocates, in various forms, sanctioning Israel until there is a genuine search for a just peace. Candidates for the 2017 legislative elections, from the En marche! movement, were disinvested after protests from the CRIF or the Ligue internationale contre le racisme et l'antisémitisme (LICRA), their positions taken in the past having been deemed too critical of Israel. Clearly, Macron did not want to antagonize the CRIF ahead of the elections. Now that he's president, his attitude doesn't seem to be changing.

At the start of the 2014 academic year, I was contacted by the Lilas public library to give a lecture there in the spring on "Conflicts in the world". It's always interesting to give a talk in the suburbs and listen to the audience's reactions. After a slight hesitation, due to the fear of overloading my schedule, I accepted. A few days before the conference, I contacted the departments again to find out about the logistical conditions. I was told that, due to the upcoming departmental elections, the hall was no longer available and the conference would have to be postponed. At first, I was delighted. After all, I'm not short of conferences, and blocking my diary at the end of the evening isn't always a pleasant prospect. That said, it's also essential to fulfill one's function as an educator. But the explanation doesn't seem entirely sincere. So I call my contact, who, very embarrassed, gives me the runaround. He explains that perhaps, since there's a joint library service in the region, I could give my talk in Bagnolet afterwards. I'm more and more intrigued. I start asking around. Eventually, I found out that the mayor of Les Lilas, Daniel Guiraud, who is running for the departmental elections, had asked that the conference not take place after being approached by two Jewish community associations. The mayor's spirit of openness, undoubtedly very "Charlie", is apparently limited; in reality, Mr. Guiraud has shown an uncommon degree of cowardice. And above all, how can it be that a conference in front of a hundred or so people, which is not mainly about the Middle East conflict—at the time it was Ukraine that was occupying people's minds—can seem so dangerous that a mayor prevents it, to the great displeasure of the library managers, because it might upset two community associations. Who, in this case, lends itself to communitarianism? Who gives Jewish organizations such power that their demands must be met immediately? Mr. Guiraud also gave in, and of course he did so for electoral reasons.

When the elected representatives of the city of Paris, regardless of their political stripe, issue a vow condemning the BDS campaign, adopting the arguments put forward by the CRIF, are they not acting on the basis of the supposed electoral weight of the Jewish community, which is supposed to constitute a bloc of support for the Israeli government? When Christian Estrosi, Éric Ciotti, Claude Goasguen or Jean-Marie Le Guen make enamored statements about Israel, is this the result of long-term strategic thinking or immediate electoral calculations? The examples could be multiplied. The paradox of the Jewish vote lies in the fact that it is both denied and overestimated, taken into consideration in practice (particularly during election campaigns)[47] without ever being mentioned publicly. On the other hand, a

---

47. Laurent BINET, in his book *Rien ne se passe comme prévu* (Grasset, 2012), tells the inside story of François Hollande's 2012 election campaign. He explains, among other things, that François Hollande had accepted a lunch with BHL "because he is a prescriber among Jews" (*sic*).

They Voted

candidate who takes a stand for the recognition of Palestine is immediately denounced as seeking an Arab community vote, even though he or she is simply taking a position in line with international law.

It is sometimes said that the weight of Jews is limited electorally and out of all proportion within society and the media. The famous "Jewish lobby" is said to be pulling the strings in France, more or less clandestinely. Is discussing the existence of such a lobby tantamount to anti-Semitism? In the USA, the answer would be no. In France, the answer is yes. The USA officially recognizes lobbies, France does not. But that doesn't mean they don't exist. You can talk about the agricultural lobby, the teachers' lobby, the cab drivers' lobby, the automobile lobby, the wine lobby, etc., without any problem. One reason for this is that, in the not-too-distant past, anti-Semites have resorted, to the point of nausea, to denouncing a "Jewish lobby" that controls France or attempts to do so. To speak of a "Jewish lobby" is in fact a shortcut, a convenience of language for some and the mask of anti-Semitism for others. Whenever I'm confronted with this question, I always explain that there is no such thing as a "Jewish lobby", simply because French Jews hold a variety of positions, including on the Israeli-Palestinian conflict. Following my initial note, I noted a diversity of appreciation among Jews on this subject that my contempteurs of course ignored. There were as many Jews among those who attacked me as among those who supported me. French Jewish community institutions are exercising a double injunction: asking their fellow Jews to show unfailing solidarity with

Israel, while at the same time protesting that Jews and Israelis can be equated.

Palestine solidarity associations include many Jews. While there is no such thing as a "Jewish lobby", there is a pro-Israeli lobby whose mission is to shield the Israeli government from criticism, whatever its behavior. This lobby is very diverse, since French Jewish institutions include personalities from all walks of life. Some are Jewish, others are not. Still others see Israel as a nation belonging to the Western camp, facing hostility from the Muslim world. Some may be Jewish, others may have Jews in their family circle, while others are reacting to the torments experienced by this people in history. Finally, there are those who, at the limit of anti-Semitic reasoning, believe that it is better to be on the side of power and therefore of the Jews, thus mentally practicing the amalgam they publicly denounce. There are Zionist anti-Semites who prefer to see Jews over there rather than here, or who hate Arabs even more than Jews. These Zionist anti-Semites admire the way Jews treat Arabs.

The confusion between anti-Semitism, anti-Zionism and criticism of the Israeli government does not stem from an error of judgment: it's a well-thought-out strategy. Quite simply, it consists in banning, by means of guilt-tripping or threats, any criticism of the Israeli government, equating it with opposition to the very existence of the Jewish state or hatred of Jews themselves. On first reflection, this assimilation does not stand up. Criticizing Vladimir Putin, Donald Trump, Xi Jinping, does not entail the risk of being considered hateful towards the United States or Americans, or of having racist contempt for Russians or Chinese. In the former case even, a criticism will often be seen as an adherence to the true values of America betrayed by Trump. So criticizing a government is not the same as opposing the state it runs.

Anti-Semitism and anti-Zionism are also different: the former is the hatred of the Jewish people or Jews, while the latter is the refusal of Jews to have a state. Yet historically, many Jews were anti-Zionists for religious reasons, because they felt that creating a state for Jews was contrary to God's will[48] or because their left-wing convictions recommended social and political transformation in the country they were in, and they did not define themselves primarily as Jews[49].

Manuel Valls largely comforted Jewish institutions by taking up this equation between anti-Zionism, anti-Semitism and criticism of the Israeli government, notably during the 2014 bombardment of Gaza. It was a major political success for Jewish institutions to see the Prime Minister of the French Republic take up their argument almost word for word. It is to be feared that this contributed to a "political closure".

---

48. See Yakov M. RABKIN, *In the Name of Torah. Une histoire de l'opposition juive au sionisme*, Presses de l'université Laval, Québec (Canada), 2004; see also Yakov M. Rabkin, "L'opposition juive au sionisme", *La Revue internationale et stratégique*, 2004/4 (n° 56). p. 17-23.
49. Dominique NATANSON, "Après la déclaration Balfour, l'antisionisme du Bund polonais dans l'entre-deux guerres", July 15, 2017, to be read on the website of the Union juive française pour la paix (UJPF), at: http://www.ujfp.org/spip.php?article5743.

Théo Klein felt that events in the Middle East had provoked a feeling of anguish and a desire to show unwavering solidarity with Israel: "I fear a ghetto complex. This idea that the outside world is hostile to us. As soon as we see hostility everywhere, we create that hostility[50]."

---

50. *Le Monde*, December 4, 2001.

For Sale

In March 2003, before the outbreak of the Iraq war, the website Proche-Orient.info devoted an article to "the tour of Arab countries: Qatar, United Arab Emirates, Iran, Syria", which I was supposed to have carried out in the space of a few weeks with "hallucinatory frenzy". I had in fact visited the United Arab Emirates in January 2002 and February 2003, one of these trips at the invitation of the French embassy, and Iran in March 2003, but had not been to Syria or Qatar. It's hard to call it a "frenzy". In the light of the Iraq war, it didn't seem altogether out of the ordinary to visit the Gulf states—for professional reasons, I often travel to all parts of the world. The article went on to state that, "from diplomatic sources, we have learned that Mr. Boniface was simply motivated by the need to raise some money and support in the Middle East to enable his office to survive the arrival of the Right in power". A rather comical reproach, given that Proche-Orient.info was in fact financed by ardent supporters of Israel, and never broke even.

The article continued, "Boniface's revisionist research lab needs to find new funding to expand its activities."

The delirium didn't stop there: "The IRIS staff simply understood that the black gold of the Gulf States would be a useful means of coping with the future. All this, of course, while also acting as intermediaries for wealthy French arms companies to advance certain juicy equipment contracts with Arab countries that have only one desire: to bring down Israel. There is no doubt that our "Sirven of strategy[51]" will one day have to answer to the peace camp and certainly to the judges of the new International Criminal Court."

So here I am, head of a revisionist institute, arms dealer threatened with referral to the ICC! Pure delirium! But widely circulated...

Between July 2001 and March 2003, I visited the United Arab Emirates twice and Iran once. Never to Syria or Qatar, as Elisabeth Schemla mentioned. But over the same period, I visited Belgium eight times, Switzerland six times, Germany three times, Russia and Spain three times, Taiwan once, Greece, the UK, Portugal, the USA, Cuba, Monaco, South Korea, India, Mali and Morocco. To say the least, my "tropism" for the Gulf countries is fairly limited and not at all frenetic.

But this frivolous, misleading, delusional and slanderous article was not to stand alone.

These attacks expanded on a familiar argument: "paid for by the Arabs". Arabs, especially in the Gulf, are rich and can afford to pay whoever they want. There's something reassuring about

---

51. In reference to Alfred Sirven, implicated in the Elf scandal.

The Anti-Semite

this argument. If I criticize the Israeli government, it can't be as a result of reasoning or analysis, but because I'm paid to. This avoids self-questioning and allows for comfortable detestation. Never far away, Frédéric Encel obviously picked up on the attacks, on the website Proche-Orient.info. In August 2004, he referred to my "aversion to Zionism and Israel", which he said could be explained by "my closeness to the Gulf petro-monarchies". When I opposed the Iraq war in 2003, this time I was accused of being "paid by Saddam". From 2010 onwards, I was accused of being paid by Qatar, because I didn't consider Qatar's hosting of the World Cup to be illegitimate, nor the Emir's visit to Gaza in 2009 to announce his help in rebuilding the territory destroyed by a war waged by Israel. While it's true that Qatar has been generous with some people, I was not one of them. Strangely enough, many of the people quoted in Chesnot and Malbrunot's book[52] have never been bothered... It's true that they have always spoken out in favor of Israeli policy. But the rumor, by dint of being repeated—even though I have criticized the kafala system, the fate of emigrants, the imprisonment of a poet—has become, for some, a certainty... The laughable thing about this slanderous argument is that it is often relayed by people who are themselves agents of influence for Israel, and owe their careers in part to this status[53].

---

52. Christian CHESNOT, Georges Malbrunot, *Nos très chers émirs*, Michel Lafon, Paris, 2016.
53. Frédéric Encel, for example, has no stable official source of income. The multiple academic titles he puts forward only correspond to a few hours of teaching a year, and don't allow him to make a living. This does not arouse curiosity.

This accusation of being paid by the Arabs is ironic in more ways than one. Firstly, because it is doubly false. Not only was I not paid by the Arabs, but on the contrary, I paid for having supported a cause purely out of conviction. Supporting the Palestinians' right to self-determination, based on the balance of power in Western societies in general and French society in particular, doesn't earn you anything; on the contrary, it costs you a lot, both personally and professionally. And I paid a double price as an individual and as founder and director of IRIS, since not only was I attacked, but so was the institute. Had I been a "mere" academic, the price would have been less heavy. Secondly, insofar as those who accuse me of taking positions out of self-interest very often organize their own careers by positioning themselves in favor of Israel, which at least assures them the support of community institutions, and sometimes even "material incentives". Finally, by taking part in a cause that is becoming increasingly difficult to defend: indeed, we may well wonder whether the two-state solution is still possible today, as the dissensions among the representatives of the Palestinian people, between the clientelistic practices of the Palestinian Authority and the repressive nature of Hamas, are problematic.

The pro-Palestinian lobby is in fact non-existent. Anyone who criticizes the Palestinian Authority risks absolutely nothing. Who got into professional trouble for criticizing Yasser Arafat, Mahmoud Abbas or Hamas? No one has! You can even make blithely racist statements about Arabs or Muslims and get away with it. If a supporter of Israel is attacked, even for facts that have nothing to do with the Middle East conflict, he or she will be defended. We'll let it be known that the community is concerned.

When I was personally attacked or when IRIS almost disappeared, I obviously received signs of solidarity from the Palestinian delegation. But they were not in a position to protest to the state authorities, and even less to the media, who questioned me. The inferiority of weight is internalized.

While Arab peoples in solidarity with the Palestinian cause are grateful to Western experts who dare to speak out on the subject without fear, Arab governments, despite their concerted declarations of solidarity, feel little concern for the Palestinian cause. Palestine is an occupied country that held free elections long before the "Arab Spring", which annoyed Arab monarchical or authoritarian republican regimes. Solidarity between Arab countries is more a slogan than a reality. And the solidarity of Arab regimes for a Western intellectual who might get into trouble for speaking out on the subject is a fiction.

In 2014, François Hollande was scheduled to travel to Israel and Palestine. The French executive is now careful not to go to Israel without making at least one detour to Palestine, in order to demonstrate equal treatment. But this is purely optical. When the head of state travels, there is always a delegation of guests. The Élysée had asked the embassy of the Palestinian Authority and the CRIF (a true parallelism would have meant asking the Israeli embassy, but no doubt the Élysée thought it was the same thing) to draw up a list of people likely to accompany the Head of State. The embassy of the Palestinian Authority asked me if I was interested, and I replied positively, preparing to adjust my schedule. This was not necessary. I was deemed too repulsive by the CRIF, and I can't be sure whether my removal from the list was the result of self-censorship by the Élysée or a veto by the CRIF. It wouldn't occur to an Élysée official to take care not to include in the delegation someone who might have irritated the Palestinians. Nor would it occur to the Palestinian Authority's ambassador in Paris to dare issue a veto against a member of the CRIF, no matter how excessive his views on the conflict.

In November 2015, Mahmoud Abbas is to be received at the Hôtel de Ville in Paris to be made an honorary citizen. As is customary, Paris City Hall protocol asked the Palestinian Authority embassy to draw up a list of guests who could attend the ceremony. I'm on the list, only to learn that Patrick Klugman has decided to remove me. Not only did no one at Paris City Hall object to this veto, but worse still, the Palestinian delegation did not demand that I be kept on the guest list. I don't go in for cocktail parties and receptions, of which I have more than enough, but this was a matter of principle. No doubt Paris City Hall wouldn't have dared make such a decision when Leïla Shahid was ambassador. In any case, the ambassador put his handkerchief in his pocket. I can't imagine a case where, for a reception for which the CRIF draws up a guest list, an elected official crosses out one of the names on the pretext that the guest has voiced criticism deemed excessive towards the Palestinian Authority. If he tried, he'd be dismissed within the hour.

There is no real pro-Palestinian or pro-Arab lobby. In any case, not able to counterbalance the pro-Israeli lobby.

The French media published endless dossiers on Russian networks in France and the way in which politicians and experts relayed Russian theses, via media such as Russia Today and Sputnik. In doing so, they lumped together those with a Gaullo-Mitterrandist vision of international affairs, those who admire Vladimir Putin's strong power and those who are supposed to be paid agents. These Russian networks do exist, but their influence on intellectual political life in France is marginal. It has nothing to do with the American network: foundations, the weight of NATO, universities and so on. No newspaper has dared to investigate Israeli networks in France. Yet they are far more powerful and influential. Tapping Vladimir Putin has never caused any problems, at least in France. There's no chance that a French research center will be threatened with closure, that an intellectual will be attacked or that there will be attempts to silence him for criticizing Vladimir Putin. On the contrary, he will have his moment of media glory. His "courage" will be hailed.

Attacking Benyamin Netanyahu is a different kettle of fish. This is where we see the true power of networks: so strong that we dare not mention them. We're likely to wait a long time before the media, which has published numerous articles and reports on Russian networks in France, does the same on Israeli networks. They are, however, far more developed... This is undoubtedly the reason for this deafening silence.

I Talk to Anyone

My line of conduct has always been the same: to favor and accept debate, including with my opponents, even though they may have insulted me in the past. There's no such thing as being in favor of peace between Israelis and Palestinians and being incapable of dialogue with someone who is or may have been your adversary in public debate. It was in this spirit that I invited Élie Barnavi to the IEP in Lille, just after the attack on me, and that I have always kept my door open to debate. Moreover, this has always been the DNA of IRIS, where debates are contradictory and guest personalities of different opinions (just like its board of directors). It's the restrictions on debate and the "entre-soi" that I shun. For the IRIS magazine, I conducted an interview with Shmuel Trigano, founder of the Observatoire du Monde Juif, who was among those who treated me harshly, and who turned out to be a fierce critic of opponents of the Israeli government[54]. It was in this spirit that I also interviewed Élie Barnavi's successor, Nissim Zvili[55], and then invited him to a conference at IRIS on January 18, 2005. Barnavi, a true man of peace with sincere convictions, accepted. This earned me some criticism from pro-Palestinian radicals who felt that I was "kowtowing" to the oppressor. However, I was simply staying true to my line. You can't call for a two-state solution and refuse all contact with Israelis committed to peace. Later, Nissim Zvili invited me to a reception organized by the Israeli Embassy on the occasion of Israel's national holiday, which I gladly accepted. Some of the guests were flabbergasted, even ulcerated, to see me there.

On June 20, 2005, IRIS organized a debate on the conflict in the Middle East at the town hall in the 11th arrondissement of Paris, with a broad and open panel of participants. In summer 2005, issue no. 58 of *La Revue internationale et stratégique*, entitled "French society and the Israeli-Palestinian conflict", was devoted to this theme. Politicians and intellectuals from all horizons and with contradictory opinions expressed themselves freely, as did Leïla Shahid and Nissim Zvili.

In the summer of 2005, François Bayrou invited me to the summer university of the UDF, the centrist party he chaired, to debate the situation in the Middle East with Rudy Salles,

---

54. Shmuel TRIGANO, "Israël et la France face à la nation", *La Revue internationale et stratégique*, 2002/3 (n° 47). p. 11-22. Théo Klein, former president of the CRIF, also spoke in this issue (p. 23-26) about his book *Le manifeste d'un juif libre*, Liana Levi, Paris, 2002.
55. Nissim ZVILI, "Renouer avec une volonté de paix", *La Revue internationale et stratégique*, 2004/2 (n° 54), p. 11-19.

MP and chairman of the France-Israel friendship group. A spirit of openness that I didn't think other political parties were capable of...

My conviction was that it was absolutely essential to preserve the space for debate on this subject, precisely because of its seriousness. To allow those who did not share the same point of view to express themselves freely, rather than fight against attempts at censorship, self-censorship, exclusion, invective and conspiracy. When debate is more or less forbidden or prevented, it takes place underground and unhealthily, or gives way to violence. In March 2002, I published an article on this subject in *Libération* with my colleague Bertrand Badie[56].

I also produced two books of debates: one with Élisabeth Schemla, the other with Gilles-William Goldnadel. Both were very different experiences.

In the first case, I was the initiator of the project: I had proposed a book of interviews to Elisabeth Schemla at the end of the colloquium that IRIS had organized at the town hall of the 11th arrondissement, which she immediately accepted. Passing for a woman of the left, her attachment to Israel was her compass. Endowed with a temperament that many recognized as impulsive and volcanic, she had attacked me with constancy, not hesitating to spread false news, driven by a sometimes slanderous impulse. She was also a gifted writer and thinker, with a solid knowledge base.

---

56. http://www.liberation.fr/tribune/2002/03/13/le-debat-pas-l-invective_396808

Although, in my opinion, she had sometimes overstepped the bounds of adversarial debate, she had also agreed to exchange views with me in sometimes lively but respectful debates. I agreed to produce this book for her publisher, Flammarion. The prospect was intellectually gratifying. At times, she was tempted to push me to modify my positions, or to take certain positions in exchange for continuing our dialogue, demanding that I condemn this or that statement, or approve another. I neither agreed nor demanded anything of him. These exchanges, mostly intellectually pleasant, had the merit of deepening my thinking. But the conclusion of the book caused a crisis, when she asked me to publicly disavow my 2001 note. I refused. In the circumstances, she explained that she could not co-author the book. I didn't give in. I'm still glad I let her choose her own publisher, who found the arguments to convince her of the need to publish the book. However, she was dropped by her sponsors when the book came out, and her website Proche-Orient.info disappeared at the same time. We did, however, have a few discussions together.

I would never have taken the initiative of proposing to write a book-debate with Me Goldnadel. His unconditional attachment to Israel is matched only by his anchorage on the right[57]. He had been one of the first to call for my head

57. Within the CRIF, Patrick Klugman and Gilles-William Goldnadel are pitted against each other: one on the left, the other on the right. In this internal struggle, playing on the repellent side I'm supposed to have for some CRIF members, the former finds it clever to apostrophize the latter by declaring that he wouldn't have shared his royalties with

in a letter to Serge Weinberg, and since then I've felt that he was more interested in polemics than debate. To my great surprise, I was invited to appear on a community radio show. The host of the show, David Reinharc, explained that he had just set up a small publishing house and was keen to maintain links between those who were opposed on the question of the Middle East. He was a hawk turned dove and was, in any case, sympathetic. He asked for my agreement in principle to produce a book of interviews with someone who would be the opposite of my convictions. To which I replied that this was my general line of conduct and that the principle suited me, even if I had questions about the solidity of his publishing house. When he suggested I do the book with Me Goldnadel, my reluctance increased. Was it worth the risk? Wouldn't we be sinking into an aggressive and sterile polemic instead of a confrontation of ideas? But refusing would have been contrary to my principles, and I had to at least give it a try. I have to admit that Gilles-William Goldnadel was absolutely correct. No one wanted to take the upper hand over the other. We were both punctual at our meetings, which took place alternately in each other's offices. Our disagreements, frank, sincere and sometimes virile, were always correct. We had diametrically opposed visions of events over there and their repercussions here, but all this was done with extreme clarity. On the other hand,

---

Pascal Boniface (in reference to the book-debate—*Sans concessions*, ed. David Reinharc, 2010—that we had done together). Not a very dignified procedure. With Gilles-William Goldnadel, our opposition was clear, frank and unequivocal, the opposite of this kind of underhand method.

I couldn't find anyone who appreciated Léo Ferré totally wrong. The response to the book was disappointing, as the publishing house was going through a very difficult period and couldn't handle the commercial and media promotion in the right conditions. But these exchanges left me with good memories and, once again, corresponded to my vision of what a democratic debate on these subjects should be[58].

Following the London bombings in 2005, I wrote an article in which I summarily explained that it was necessary to tackle not only the effects of terrorism, but also its causes, and that the Iraq war, far from having brought terrorism down, had, on the contrary, nurtured it. Marc Knobel and Richard Prasquier, two leaders of the CRIF, accused me of cultivating both the Munich and Stockholm syndromes. As I knew Mr. Knobel, I disagreed with his interpretation. He suggested a meeting with Richard Prasquier, which took place over a constructive lunch, proving that it is possible to discuss our differences calmly. Richard Prasquier was subsequently elected to the presidency of the CRIF and accepted my invitation to a colloquium on the influence of France and diversity organized by IRIS at the end of 2008[59]. Subsequently, in view of the worsening situation in the Middle East, and in order not to upset the increasingly radicalized fringe of the CRIF, he put an end to this association. Roger Cukierman, who had preceded him and succeeded him at the head of

---

58. Elisabeth Schemla reproached me, in a murderous message, for having so many debates with Jewish opponents.
59. "La diversité, un atout pour la France", *La Revue internationale et stratégique*, 2009/1 (n° 73).

the CRIF, had not spared me during his first term. When he published his book *Ni fiers ni dominateurs*, he repeated the ritual accusation that I had recommended a pro-Palestinian stance because there were more Arabs than Jews. I contacted him to protest for the umpteenth time against this accusation. To my surprise, he accepted the contact and visited me at IRIS. We had an interview, published in issue 72 of the IRIS magazine, and have remained in courteous contact ever since. We even had two pleasant lunches together, respecting each other's differences. Following a further deterioration in the climate, my colleague Jean-Paul Chagnollaud and I asked for a meeting, in a letter in which we acknowledged the difficulties created in France by the debate on the Israeli-Palestinian conflict and expressed our wish to limit its excesses. To our surprise, he agreed, and we went to the CRIF headquarters to have a discussion that would highlight our differences but also show a willingness to engage in dialogue. We came away rather satisfied. On the way home, I heard sirens wailing. It was January 7, 2015, and the appointment had been set for 11am. We were entering a completely different climate.

Over and above their own convictions, institutional leaders often have to take account of the opinions of the most radicalized fringe of their base. The latter, heated up to the point of no return, indulge in one-upmanship. I've heard them say this repeatedly, and their attitude confirms it. The Jews of France (like the Israelis) are leaning more and more to the right, but even more than this political mutation, they are becoming radicalized, afraid for their security and their future in France. Community withdrawal is becoming a reality. A vicious circle begins. The community's authorities and organic intellectuals constantly denounce the rise in anti-Semitism, both because they are convinced of it and because they want to use it to protect Israel. They heighten the fear of many Jews, who have less and less confidence in those who do not fully accept their arguments. This strategy was effective in making France less active on the question of peace between Israel and Palestine[60]. But it has widened the gap between the French, making the Israeli question a dividing line between those who unconditionally support Israel and those who criticize it[61].

My fear is that the debate will become increasingly difficult in France as the situation in the Middle East deteriorates. The opposite would be necessary. It's not that the Palestinians are without fault and/or have never made mistakes. But the occupation of one people by another, already unacceptable in the 20th century, is even more intolerable in the 21st.

---

60. Pascal BONIFACE, *Je t'aimais bien tu sais. Le monde et la France, le désamour?*, Max Milo, Paris, 2017.
61. *Id. La France malade du conflit israélo-palestinien,* Éditions Salvator, Paris, 2014.

This Wound

I could no longer live in the rue des Écouffes where I spent so many happy years. I'd probably be looked down upon by many of my Jewish neighbors, the same ones who warmly welcomed me in 1978. Yet my convictions haven't changed, whether on anti-Semitism or the Israeli-Palestinian conflict. What has changed is their state of mind. A large proportion of them have become radicalized and are quick to denounce anti-Semitism, despite the fact that anti-Semitism has generally declined in society since that time. What has also changed is the way I am perceived: yesterday, a fellow traveler; today, a dangerous adversary.

Gradually, rumor became certainty, and the accusation undeniable proof. Many people, particularly in the Jewish community, talk about the "Boniface report", which they have often read in the press or on social networks, and which recommends abandoning the Jews for the Arabs because the latter are more numerous and carry more electoral weight.

How many times have I heard "your reputation precedes you". By hammering it home on community radios and newspapers, it's not surprising that many people are—even a little—convinced of my anti-Semitism. Yet what they've heard, if not read, doesn't match what I've written or said.

The "I haven't read it but I've heard about it" aspect can even reach people who are supposed to be particularly well-informed. During the promotion of my book of interviews with Elisabeth Schemla, I met the owner of Radio Shalom, a station considered to be on the left of the community spectrum. He told me, without being shocked himself: "I haven't read your note, but I've judged you by it. That the head of a media outlet should be content with hearsay on a matter to which he attaches so much importance, without checking the accuracy of the facts, is quite astounding. On RTL, Patrick Cohen said in my presence: "For Pascal Boniface, the Jews are responsible for anti-Semitism". My arms fall off. Where on earth did he get this "information"? It's the result of hammering away in community media, forums, social networks and even the mainstream media. For example, on March 16, 2006, Jacques Chancel interviewed Philippe Val and BHL on I-Télé.

The first declares, "You'd think the Islamist lobby[62] could shake the status of the Jewish community."

BHL replies: "Obviously, and for people who can reason... there was, moreover, in the Socialist Party... a few years ago... There's a guy called Pascal Boniface who handed out

---

62. Apparently, talking about the "Islamist lobby" doesn't bother anyone.

a memo that was supposed to remain secret, but which was obviously made public, in which he said to the Socialist leaders, 'Watch out, because today you're doing the Jewish community a favor, but are you fully aware that there are many more Muslim voters, and that in a few years' time it's going to be… no contest'. So of course there are always people who calculate like that. There are always people who say, yes, we reason in terms of communities, we reason in terms of terrorist risks, the attitude in the cartoons affair was typical."

BHL, who knows perfectly well the contents of my note and was behind Serge Weinberg's resignation from the IRIS Board of Directors, was lying through his teeth. I therefore asked for a right of reply, which I was unable to obtain. I thought of suing, but it would have been long and costly… I'm not a billionaire.

To tell the truth, it doesn't hurt me much to be disliked by BHL. What hurts me more is the feeling of rejection I inspire among many fellow Jews because BHL and other disinformers have manipulated my words and presented me as an anti-Semite. I understand that this can create a feeling of anguish. Organic leaders and intellectuals insist on the rise of anti-Semitism in France (this has been the theme of every CRIF president's annual dinner speech since 2001). In 2002, Alain Finkielkraut even spoke of "the year of crystal", a theme often taken up in voluminous dossiers in the mainstream press (which has devoted relatively little to the rise of anti-Arab racism). Many Jews in France are afraid, and for some of them I have become one of the causes of their problems. In fact, my relations with many of my compatriots are altered by the false perception they have of my positions, my career and my struggles. I can arouse in advance a reflex of distrust, reticence or hostility in people who don't know me but have heard of me.

A few years ago, one of my sons—then in ninth grade— told me that one of her classmates would like to do the compulsory one-week internship at IRIS that students do in their last year of secondary school. She's passionate about geopolitics. I agreed. After a few weeks, when I hadn't heard from her, I asked how things were going. He replied that she had given up because of my anti-Semitism. This must be what she heard at home. I take note of this decision, saying to myself that it would be a pity if young Jews didn't want to associate with my son because of their father's presumed anti-Semitism. Fortunately, the bonds of friendship between the two resisted this prejudice to such an extent that she finally decided to spend her week's internship at IRIS. She had a thoroughly satisfying week, seeing for herself how people of all faiths worked together in harmony.

Another such surprise: one day, while talking with another of my sons, he tells me that one of his best friends thinks I'm more or less anti-Semitic. I've known this young man since early childhood, and he often came to the house. When he moved to Strasbourg from Paris, we even spent vacations together, and we still meet, but in his new city, many Jewish friends have influenced him.

As a student at ESSEC, my third son applied for a job when he finished his studies. He applied for a position with a major consulting firm. After four successive successful interviews, with just as many different people, and just as he was about to close, the HR manager called him and told him that, after some research, they were embarrassed by articles implicating him in connection with a video: "You understand that we have an image to defend." My son replies that if they're sensitive to the propaganda of the pro-Israeli far right, there's not much he can do about it, and he's not that keen to get involved with them. Things ended there and he went to work elsewhere. What happened? Three and a half years earlier, my son had taken part in a comedy competition for business school students: the Campus Comedy Tour. Among many other things, he had talked about the Middle East conflict. His sketch may not have earned him a place at the Olympia, but it certainly didn't land him in criminal court either. Frédéric Encel, who plays the rigorous academic but uses methods worthy of an agent, had sent an indignant e-mail to a hundred journalists and the Shoah Memorial! "If you want to get stomach cramps, listen to Boniface's son at ESSEC. Worse than his father, it exists: his son Corentin! A display of commonplaces, misunderstandings, an intellectual level of a primate." No one, of course, had bothered to listen to the sketch or heard an anti-Semitic slur. If they had, the law would have been quick to intervene. Only the extremist sites JSSNews and Dreuz info had taken up Frédéric Encel's slander. But this trace remains. Attacking the son in a slanderous way to get at the father—we can only appreciate the dignity of the method.

Medical appointment. At the end of the consultation, the doctor, whose origins had not escaped me (because of his name) tells me: "You're much nicer in person than on television. I point out that it's hard to smile when you're talking about serious subjects. He agrees, but points out that it's what I say in public that can provoke reticence. I ask him to clarify what he means, or to quote precisely what he said that might have given rise to negative feelings. I ask him if he blames me for what I said or for what he heard. If we get to the heart of the matter, we agree on the need for peace between Israelis and Palestinians, and on the difficulties that the military occupation of a people automatically creates. He is very attached to Israel and sincerely in favor of peace. He tells me he's happy to have met me and to have dispelled preconceived ideas about me. With people of good faith, direct contact always makes it possible to explain things. We don't agree on everything, but I don't suspect him of being a supporter of colonization. He doesn't think I'm obsessed with the Jews, either. If I say to myself on the way out that this is extremely comforting, it would nevertheless take some time to have thousands of individual interviews...

Should this mistrust lead me, in order to prevent any unpleasantness, to avoid entering into professional or personal relationships, or even making contact, with Jewish people? I absolutely refuse to enter this vicious circle. If there are misunderstandings, first try to clear them up. If they persist, at least I've tried. And there are so many pleasant surprises that it's worth having a few disappointments.

Just as it's Over, it Starts Again

One of the reasons I set up IRIS was to benefit from a framework that allowed me to express myself freely on international issues. Of course, if I had remained an individual teacher and/or researcher, I would have retained this freedom. But it seemed useful and more enjoyable to belong to a collective. Strategic and defense issues are underdeveloped at university, and I didn't have a university research laboratory to link up with. In short, setting up an association seemed the best way to guarantee this freedom and enrich my thinking. But this springboard can become a trap. I am also responsible for the structure and those who work within it, and if I cannot be prevented from expressing myself, it is quite conceivable to attack IRIS to dissuade me from continuing to express myself freely. And so it was. Even in a democratic country, expressing oneself without constraint on matters of state always poses a problem. I know colleagues, including academics, who are therefore not judged by the political authorities, but who nonetheless observe a certain prudence, even caution, in the judgments they may express.

In 1993, IRIS, which had just come into being, was very fragile. I was undoubtedly linked to the Socialist Party, and it would have been easy for the new government to turn off the meagre tap of subsidies we had at our disposal. IRIS's visibility was low enough for this to happen without a ripple. But this was not the case, and the few funds we had at the time were maintained unchanged. Pierre Lellouche even intervened on our behalf, despite belonging to the Gaullist party of the time. Worse still, in 1995, Jacques Chirac, who had just been elected President of the Republic, took two major foreign policy decisions: France's reintegration into NATO and the resumption of nuclear testing. These decisions represented a complete break with the actions of François Mitterrand, and were central to the new executive. I criticized both in the media. This in no way affected working relations with the Ministry of Defense and Foreign Affairs, nor the level of funding IRIS received. In short, criticizing major, emblematic decisions on sovereign issues didn't cause me any specific problems. On the other hand, criticizing the actions of a foreign government, on the basis of respect for international law, almost caused the demise of IRIS.

On numerous occasions, BHL has attacked high-level politicians to whom he has direct access, saying that I was "infrequentable". According to this label, no one could be near me or bear my presence. Quite simply, it's a clear call for a boycott. The same man who is outraged when NGOs propose a boycott of agricultural products from Israeli settlements in the Palestinian territories, considers it perfectly normal for one of his compatriots to be ostracized for criticizing a foreign country to which he feels particularly attached. For him, as for others, I'm less important than an orange produced in the colonies. When his play *Hotel Europe* came out, I made a bet—admittedly not a very risky one—that it would get Hollywood-style promotion, but that audiences wouldn't follow. His play was indeed a flop. Annoyed by my ironic remark (humor doesn't seem to be his style), at the microphone of Frédéric Haziza on Radio J, on November 16, 2015, BHL evoked a "little Boniface, Ramadan, Soral, Dieudonné sect" which, according to him, makes up "a kind of ideological nebula". It's amusing to see the man who readily denounces conspiracy theories resort to them himself.

But that wasn't enough. He went on: "Boniface, I don't know who he is exactly, but from what I've been told, he's got some kind of little French think tank, subsidized by the taxpayer."

Haziza took the opportunity to agree with him: "[...] and in particular by the Quai d'Orsay".

BHL's response: "He can indeed say things like that, I don't even understand what he's talking about... If this kind of thing is really subsidized by the Quai d'Orsay, it deserves to be questioned. We should ask ourselves, and we should ask the main people involved."

Apart from the fact that, once again, BHL is telling a big lie when he claims not to know me, this was an attempt to dry up IRIS's funding and contacts.

After 2003, Pierre Lellouche was about to siege the members of the IRIS Board of Directors belonging to his political family, demanding their immediate resignation. When Arthur Paecht turned him down, he didn't hesitate to ask his son, who worked in the defense industry, about the subject, during a meeting where the unfortunate man was not really in a position to answer a member of parliament. He also tried his luck with Alain Marsaud who, incidentally, does not share my views on the Israeli-Palestinian conflict, or on other subjects, but considers it necessary to confront ideas.

After the publication of my book La France malade du conflit israélo-palestinien[63], Frédéric Haziza went wild on Twitter, posting a multitude of abusive tweets about me, likening me to Alain Soral and/or Dieudonné, and insisting on my "Jewish obsession". He had already regularly attacked me in 2001 after my note. The consistency and duration of his attacks can only be questioned. Of course, he made sure I couldn't be invited to appear on LCP—AN—and he regularly challenged me in front of his guests on Radio J—no less than six times in two months!—using the tactic of asking his guests biased questions so that they would publicly condemn me in order not to displease the interviewer and his audience. He even went so far as to blame me for the hostage-taking and killing at the Hyper Casher store at Porte de Vincennes. This prompted a petition against him, signed

---

63. Pascal BONIFACE, *La France malade du conflit israélo-palestinien, op.cit.*

by numerous Jewish personalities[64] and a response from André Schmer, former FTP-MOI resistance fighter[65]. Once again, proof that the divide is not where it seems. But that didn't stop him from continuing his relentless undermining. It was no longer enough for him to attack me; he also had to get to IRIS to make it disappear. He devoted remarkable time and energy to this task. He began to make the rounds of the various members of the Board of Directors, telling them how much he loathed me and how anomalous it was for Republicans to remain linked to me and the institute I headed. He also published two almost identical echoes in the front pages of the weeklies *Le Point* and *L'Express,* with the complicity of journalists who take part in his programs on LCP—AN, according to which "A minister close to Manuel Valls warns: IRIS is a research institute, not a committed NGO. In his sights is Pascal Boniface, director of IRIS and reputedly pro-Palestinian, who described a manual against racism and anti-Semitism published by LICRA and hosted on the French Education Ministry's website as biased pro-Israeli preaching. The ruling prompted the resignation of Patrick Bloche, PS deputy for Paris, from the IRIS board of directors."

---

64. https://www.change.org/p/l-opinion-publique-stop-%C3%A0-la-chasse-aux-sorci%C3%A8res-soutien-%C3%A0-pascal-boniface-624c1e83-0f68-4032-88c4-5573503fdba4
65. http://leplus.nouvelobs.com/contribution/1169224-pascal-boniface-ac-cuse-d-antisemitisme-m-haziza-je-suis-juif-vous-faites-fausse-route.html

Just as it's Over, it Starts Again

Under the pretext of combating racism, the book's main aim was to present a biased view of Israel, to talk about the Israeli-Palestinian conflict from a pro-Israeli angle[66].

"What's more, a researcher from the institute has published a highly critical article on the Intelligence Act. Yet IRIS operates, in particular, thanks to hundreds of thousands of euros of public money," reminds the Minister."

Apart from the fact that, unfortunately, we don't have hundreds of thousands of euros in subsidies, we're still appalled by this kind of judgment: was it really issued by a minister? Or is it just a rumor spread by Haziza? There are several factors that make this "brief" shocking to read, and which show the intellectual and moral wretchedness of the person behind it. Since a research institute is not a committed NGO, should its researchers never take a stand on any issue? Does linking state subsidies to critical judgment on a law mean that, as in totalitarian countries, it is forbidden to criticize the government?

During the campaign for the PS primaries, for the designation of the presidential candidate, before the second round which was to oppose Benoît Hamon to Manuel Valls, Frédéric Haziza received the latter at the microphone of Radio J, on January 26, 2017. He then put a few pieces back into the machine:

F. Haziza: "[...] This reminds us of a note published by Pascal Boniface in April 2001. At the time, he was developing the idea that since Muslims in France far outnumber Jews,

---

66. http://leplus.nouvelobs.com/contribution/1320265-la-licra-son-livre-contre-le-racisme-et-l-antisemitisme-un-preche-partial-pro-isrealien.html

the PS should criticize Israel more, not because the cause was just, but because otherwise the coming elections might be compromised [...] What do you think of this rapprochement, this parallel drawn by your friends?"

Mr. Valls: "Funny thesis [...]".

Yes, funny indeed, if it were mine. But in fact it's pure disinformation, which Frédéric Haziza knows all too well when he brings Mr. Valls into it.

FH: "That was Pascal Boniface's thesis."

MV: "Funny thesis, precisely [...] funny thesis [...] I've always been amazed that Pascal Boniface still finds an attentive ear among certain leaders [...]".

FH: "Do you mean PS leaders or State leaders?"

MV: "Managers in general. But that poses a real problem. It's his freedom to write that, it's his problem [...]"

FH: "April 2001, huh [...]"

MV: "But that can't be... Er... That can't be an acceptable thesis. Because if it is, it means we accept the fragmentation of French society into communities. It means that the communitarian model is imposed."

FH: "You say you're surprised by Pascal Boniface's audience. How do you explain it?"

MV: "But that's for you to explain [...] I'm not sure that this audience is extremely powerful [...] But you have to be careful with these theses, because they are devious, they instill division. They instill fractures, they are ambiguous. There can be no ambiguity whatsoever in this area."

Manuel Valls' comments are surprising in more ways than one. First of all, if this note had been so shocking,

Just as it's Over, it Starts Again

why would he have sent me a handwritten letter of support during the 2002 controversy[67]? Why did he agree to be a member of the IRIS Board of Directors? Why did we stay in touch for so long? And what about Michel Rocard, who had also always criticized Israeli colonization? Isn't it strange that he condemned communitarianism at the microphone of Frédéric Haziza on Radio J? Didn't he rather reinforce it, by systematically adopting the arguments and language of the official institutions of the Jewish community, both on internal issues and on the Israeli-Palestinian conflict?

In the November 10, 2017 issue of *Marianne,* Manuel Valls went into overdrive. He declared: "I consider, for example, that what the academic Pascal Boniface has been writing for years poses a real problem. I have in fact referred this matter to the Ministers of Foreign Affairs and the Armed Forces, who fund IRIS, even though he does not speak on behalf of IRIS."

So Mr. Valls is proposing that an institute employing thirty people should be ostracized from government service, because the center's director holds positions he doesn't like. In what kind of regime is this behavior possible? Does he realize the implications of his remarks?

It's absolutely mind-boggling!

Manuel Valls, without realizing it, takes up José MillánAstray's Francoist slogan: "Death to intelligence, *Viva la muerte!*"

____

67. See Appendix 4.

Justice will Follow
in our Triumphant Footsteps

In May 2004, Malek Boutih, giving an interview to the pro-Israeli site primo-Europe, responded to the remark that "all the same, the Jews of France have not forgotten the Boniface report": "I'll have you know that Boniface has resigned from the PS leadership. We don't want the PS to be involved in this kind of relationship with society, i.e. to go in the direction of communitarianism."

In a letter sent on June 15, I replied that it was astonishing that he should have perceived a communitarian approach in my note, referring him to read it in full. I added that the accusation of communitarianism levelled at me was not innocent and was the result of manipulation, pointing out that I would appreciate it in future if he did not accuse me unjustifiably. I received no reply to this letter until the newspaper *Technikart* published a new interview with Mr. Boutih.

On December 2, 2004, he declared: "Pascal Boniface? He did well to get out of the PS! I've stepped up to the plate to break this shift in anti-Zionism, from a position of political radicalism to a kind of racism. It's one of the common traits of all anti-Semites: they don't assume, they camouflage their anti-Semitism with a theorization that doesn't hold water."

Mr. Boutih was president of SOS Racisme and a key figure in the debate. He strengthened the structural links between SOS Racisme and the UEJF, chaired by Patrick Klugman. I was beginning to tire of these attacks. So I consulted my lawyer and friend, Jean-Yves Halimi. He advised me to lodge a complaint for defamation, which I did. The tribunal de grande instance and then the court of appeal ruled in my favor. In the judgment of October 31, 2006, we read the following passage: "This document, with its measured tone, constitutes an analysis, which may be approved or criticized, of the situation in the Middle East as well as the way it is perceived in France, and proposes that the Socialist Party adopt a position that is more just, in the eyes of its author, and more in line with the well-understood interests of the two communities particularly concerned by the conflict on French territory. Only mentioning in passing and in order to better convince its addressees of the considerations linked to the relative electoral weight of the said communities, this document is clearly distorted by the summary and partial summary [which has been] proposed [...].] Finally, Pascal Boniface's suggestion that the political party of which he was a member should make up its mind, on a subject that is sensitive because of the ethical, historical, domestic and international political issues it raises, not on the basis of the rule of law and the collective interest, but on the basis of electoral considerations tinged with anti-Semitism that would appear to lie behind radical anti-Zionism, is contrary to the party's honor and esteem."

On July 5, 2007, the Court of Appeal upheld the conviction for defamation, "considering that the defense is not entitled to invoke the debate of opinion, such an imputation exceeding by nature the limits of the debate of opinion".

In one paragraph, she reminded us: "Pascal Boniface in fact refers to the electoral weight of the Jewish community and that of the community of Arab or Muslim origin, Technikart's brief and biased summary distorts Pascal Boniface's much more nuanced analyses of the situation in the Middle East and the question of anti-Semitism [...] Considering that Technikart has summarized and distorted both Malek Boutik's remarks and Pascal Boniface's analyses; that in any case, political polemic cannot justify the seriousness of the accusation made."

Justice was officially served. The TGI and the Court of Appeal officially recognized that accusing me of having recommended a position more favorable to the Palestinians because there were more Arabs than Jews in France was an untruth. In a state governed by the rule of law, this should have put an end to the controversy. But for my opponents, res judicata only has value when it suits them. For some, malicious rumors are stronger than the justice of the Republic.

At the end of 2005, a CRIF official told me that a very nasty maneuver was being mounted against me. Although he disagrees with me, he cannot, as a matter of morality, condone this type of method. In the monthly *Balkans-Infos, which has* nothing to do with the Middle East, an article reports that I caused a scandal at the Rendez-vous de l'histoire in Blois in October, by declaring: "Y en a que pour les Juifs; ici, à ce Salon, la moitié des auteurs sont juifs, la plupart des conférenciers sont le; y en a marre des Juifs, ça fait soixante ans qu'il nous en emm... avec la Shoah! They hold all the levers of command, and it was they who organized the Iraq war in 2003, in order to establish a greater Israel" [...] The audience was stunned and scandalized. The individual was identified as Pascal Boniface, author of a book entitled *Est-il permis de critiquer Israël?* He was taken to task by one of the hostesses, seemed to calm down, and then repeated: "It's a scandal! We can't say another word against the Jews! These people are using the history of their persecution to justify a greater Israel and forbid us to criticize this country.

If I had made such remarks in a place as busy as the Rendez-vous de l'histoire dinner in Blois, it would not have gone unnoticed. The scandal would have been legitimately enormous! How, then, could we find a rational explanation for this operation? The strategy had to be as follows: publish the information in a confidential newsletter (*Balkans-Infos*, with an estimated circulation of four hundred copies), which had little chance of reaching me, let the three-month period pass during which you can lodge a complaint for defamation, then relay this "information" widely and with impunity. A lie repeated a hundred times doesn't become the truth, but it can influence perceptions. So I decided to lodge a complaint against the *Balkans-Infos* newspaper. On the day of the trial, the director of the publication, a dignified old gentleman, arrived accompanied by the author of the article, dressed rather scruffily, to use a euphemism, and with an uncertain demeanor. He explains that he is an outside contributor who has simply published two previous articles on B'nai B'rith conferences. The author's comments were so incoherent that the presiding judge called for a psychiatric examination before ruling on the case, and postponed the trial! Clearly, this person could not have been invited to the official Rendez-vous de l'histoire dinner. Who had manipulated him into writing this type of paper? It's a pity that the investigators didn't investigate further. But I did wonder: the article appeared in the same year as Frédéric Encel's exfiltration from the Rendez-vous de l'histoire, at Esther Benbassa's request, for usurpation of academic titles: wasn't this revenge on his part? In any case, he could have spotted this unfortunate, bewildered young man at one of the colloquia of B'nai B'rith, the movement that supports Encel and which Encel frequents assiduously.

In July 2008, *Balkans-infos* and the author of the article were found guilty of defamation by the criminal court. November saw the start of the Salon d'Alger affair.

I was invited to take part in a debate and give a talk at the Salon International du Livre in Algiers. When asked about the "poor image of Muslims in France" and the "responsibility of the Jewish lobby" in this matter, I replied that there was no such thing. French Jews have contrasting opinions, both on Islam and on the Israeli-Palestinian conflict. On the other hand, there are a number of media figures of diverse origins who contribute to conveying a negative image of Muslims: I cite BHL, Alain Finkielkraut, but also Philippe Val and Mohamed Sifaoui. The Arabic-language daily El-Khabar, deliberately or through incompetence, mistranslated my words and wrote that I had referred to a "Jewish lobby". Immediately, Élisabeth Lévy and Mohamed Sifaoui attacked me in their respective blogs, citing a newspaper to which they do not usually refer. The French-language Algerian press, on the other hand, correctly translated my words and emphasized that I had denied the existence of such a lobby. On his blog, Mr. Sifaoui devoted a long article to me, in which he accused me of intellectual complicity with terrorists and deplored the fact that my media appearances were giving rise to a new form of anti-Semitism. The witnesses quoted by Mr. Sifaoui were a sort of who's who of the pro-Israel lobby. They included Frédéric Encel, Caroline Fourest, Richard Prasquier, Dominique Sopo, Bernard-Henri Lévy, Jacky Mamou, Alexandra Laignel-Lavastine, Raphaël Haddad (UEJF), Patrick Klugman, Pierre-André Taguieff and Antoine Vitkine. Prasquier, Fourest, Haddad, Sopo and Klugman themselves came to the hearing to support the soldier Sifaoui. The court dismissed the case, as the passages cited as defamatory did not impute concrete acts to me, but rather attributed opinions to me. It also dismissed Mohamed Sifaoui's claims against me for reimbursement of expenses incurred.

I See the World a Bit like Seeing the Incredible

In my 2001 note, I wrote: "The intellectual terrorism of accusing those who do not accept the policies of Israeli governments (not the State of Israel) of anti-Semitism pays off in the short term, but can prove catastrophic in the medium term."

I was wrong. Seventeen years on, this intellectual terrorism is still as prevalent as ever, and as effective as ever. The continuing deterioration of the situation in the Middle East since 2000-2001 has led to an intensification of its use and, more surprisingly, an increase in its effectiveness.

What happened to me is scarcely believable. For sixteen years, the same arguments have been invoked, when a simple fifteen-second reflection can reveal their inanity. The same preconceived ideas that shouldn't stand up to scrutiny seem to be set in stone. I find it hard to believe that, in a world where knowledge, individual and/or collective reflection and the means to know and understand are increasing daily, we can still claim that criticizing a country's government is tantamount to hating it and its people. The strategy of using the fight against anti-Semitism to protect a government that combines the hard right and the extreme right has long since paid off.

After the Rue des Rosiers attack on Jo Goldenberg's restaurant in 1982, Betar militants greeted François Mitterrand, who was visiting the scene, with shouts of "Mitterrand, assassin". Israeli Prime Minister Menachem Begin declares: "The crime committed in the heart of Paris is the consequence of allusions to Oradour and of a deliberately anti-Israeli attitude—which is also anti-Jewish—in the French press and media as a whole. Once again, the streets of Paris resounded with cries of 'Death to the Jews', as they did at the time of the Dreyfus Affair."

At a time when Israel's image had been shaken by the war in Lebanon, Mr. Begin used the weapon of the fight against anti-Semitism to make his government more secure and to prohibit, through guilt, support or fear, any criticism of its actions. The method was to be used constantly thereafter, with peaks such as the resumption of the Intifada in 2001 and the Gaza war in 2014.

It's undeniable that anti-Semitic prejudice still circulates in France, particularly—but not only—in disadvantaged suburbs. Prejudice also exists in more affluent neighborhoods, but is perhaps less clearly or openly expressed, perhaps because the feeling of a "double standard" is, among other things, less prevalent there.

I'm regularly confronted with this type of prejudice when I give talks or lectures. I never use double-speak, and say the same thing no matter who my audience is. It's not only a question of principle, but also of realism: to think that double-speak could go unnoticed is an illusion, at least for those who take positions like mine. Frédéric Haziza may have said that, "as a journalist, he had always worked for Israel", BHL may have said, at a CRIF convention, that he had pushed for war in Libya with "Israel first and foremost in mind", or Frédéric Encel may have said, on a community radio station, say that when he goes to the media, he does so "above all to defend Israel" or, at a conference in Israel, that he "never criticizes Israel", even though in public he claims to be a rigorous academic, without any of them having suffered any reputational damage as a result. If I had said somewhere that the meaning of my life was the defense of Palestinians or the promotion of Arabs, my "friends" would have strongly relayed this statement, which would have definitely damaged my capacity for media exposure.

When I hear "the Zionist entity" mentioned in a meeting, I correct myself and refer to the State of Israel. You can't proclaim yourself in favor of a two-state solution and deny one of them the right to exist.

It's easy to condemn anti-Semitism on the Place du Trocadéro, at rallies attended only by the convinced, without risking contradiction. I sometimes defend Israel's right to exist within secure, recognized borders, in front of less comfortable audiences, both in France and abroad. For some, the fight against anti-Semitism is a battle, for others it's a vector for professional success, even a livelihood. Accused of anti-Semitism by some, I'm also called a "lackey of Zionism" by others, notably Alain Soral and his friends. The latter claim that I've given in, so as not to jeopardize the existence of IRIS or my income, and that real resistance fighters are braver than I am. Some extremists have criticized me for including many Jewish personalities in my book *Les intellectuels intègres*[68].

On January 6, 1970, at the end of a Council of Ministers meeting following the Cherbourg speedboat affair, the embargo on arms to Israel, which had only been partial (spare parts essential to maintaining the air force continued to be supplied), became total, a move widely criticized by the pro-Israel French press. The government spokesman declared at the time: "It is remarkable and has been noticed that Israeli influences are felt in a certain way in circles close to information[69]."

No government official could make such a statement today without being dismissed within the hour. Any politician and/ or journalist making such a statement would see his or her career immediately halted.

Beyond the persistence of an old anti-Semitism, it's certain that part of the youth and population feel antipathy towards Jews, seen as a global community controlling France,

---

68. Published by Jean-Claude Gawsewitch in 2013: Stéphane Hessel, Esther Benbassa, Rony Brauman, Alfred Grosser, Edgar Morin and Michel Wieviorka.
69. Quoted *in* Alain Gresh, Hélène Aldeguer, *Un chant d'amour : Israël-Palestine, une histoire française, op.cit.*

the press and the economy. When people tell me that the Jews control the media, I correct them, but I also engage in dialogue. I don't think that an outraged injunction is the best response. Requiring someone to shut up immediately after uttering such nonsense, or excluding them from the conversation, won't change their mind. Discussion often does. All the more so as I enjoy a certain aura in these circles, which praise my integrity. So I think I'm doing my bit in the fight against anti-Semitism.

Faced with an anti-Semitic cliché about Jews and the media, I'd like to start by pointing out the diversity of positions on the Middle East conflict among Jews, many of whom are at the forefront of solidarity with the Palestinian cause. To claim that one community controls the whole is simply an untruth. It's undeniable that the media are more sensitive to the accusation of anti-Semitism than to that of anti-Muslim racism, to avoid using the dirty word "Islamophobia". But no one is fooled. The media fame of figures such as BHL and Imam Chalghoumi is proof that anything and everything can be said in support of Israel. To say that Jews control the media is an anti-Semitic statement, but to assert that they don't have privileged access to it, especially in comparison with the Muslim community, is a denial of reality. Similarly, it's stupid to say that Jews control the political class, but who can deny that politicians are quicker to react to anti-Semitic aggression than to aggression against Muslims? The fact that the inter-ministerial delegate for the fight against racism, Gilles Clavreul, emphasizes the primary importance of the fight against anti-Semitism over other forms of racism, that he has largely confused the defense of the Israeli government with the fight against anti-Semitism, that he neither hired nor involved in the work of the DILCRA people who might have been critical of the Israeli government, that he never wanted to receive Jewish pacifist associations and that he fiercely opposed attempts at autonomous organization by Arabs and Muslims, was a real gift to the initiators of nauseating rumors about the occult power of the Jews. Don't the high-profile institutional Jewish associations, which lobby political leaders to obtain support for Israel or to refrain from criticizing it, and which intervene heavily in court cases to make their point, help to fuel fears?

Unfortunately, anti-Semitism persists in France. It has nothing to do with the scale it had before the Second World War, or even up to the end of the 1960s. In the early 2000s, some saw fit to develop the concept of "left-wing anti-Semitism". The left is generally associated with the fight against racism, but there's nothing automatic about that: you can be left-wing, vote that way, claim to be left-wing and still be anti-Semitic. You can also be an anti-Muslim racist in the same circumstances. The academic Michel Dreyfus has written a very interesting and learned book on the subject[70]. But the development of the rhetoric of "left-wing anti-Semitism" in the early 2000s was really aimed at marginalizing those on the left who criticized Israel, even though they were used to supporting it.

---

70. Michel DREYFUS, *L'antisémitisme à gauche. Histoire d'un paradoxe, de 1830 à nos jours*, La Découverte, Paris, 2009, enlarged reprint 2011.

I think nothing would have pleased some of my adversaries more than for me to become truly anti-Semitic. That, after taking unfair blows from all sides, I should overreact and launch into inflammatory statements, making my accusers the sole representatives of the Jews of France. Such a drift would have justified their initial accusations and delighted them. As Guillaume Weill-Raynal wrote: "If Boniface is the man to silence, it's precisely because of the moderate nature of his positions on the Middle East conflict, which makes him more dangerous for extremists of all stripes. If he were truly anti-Semitic, we'd leave him alone[71]."

Of course, the focus would have been on the facts, not the causes. I even wonder if some people aren't reassured when they encounter real anti-Semites, because it justifies their massive retaliation, instead of targeting with surgical strikes. If I hadn't had solid convictions, if my intellectual training, when these attacks happened, hadn't already been quite consistent, if I hadn't been surrounded by sure and faithful friends, if I hadn't received so many expressions of solidarity, many of them from French Jews, if my close family circle hadn't been totally supportive, perhaps I would have drifted. In fact, it would have been the attacks accusing me of being anti-Semitic that would have pushed me into this serious slip; a self-fulfilling prophecy, in short. Fortunately, I escaped this and continue to fight against all forms of racism, including anti-Semitism. I don't put the fight against

---

71. Guillaume WEILL-RAYNAL, "Qui veut la peau de Pascal Boniface", *L'Obs*, February 4, 2009.

I See the World a Bit like Seeing the Incredible

anti-Semitism above other forms of racism, but I don't forget it either. There can be no hierarchy in this area.

In the fight against anti-Semitism, I'm an ally of Jewish community organizations, both official and unofficial. They know it. But they don't see me as such. Because the most important thing for them is to prevent any criticism of the Israeli government. And here I'm an adversary, especially as I'm not anti-Semitic.

Some people accuse me, if not of being anti-Semitic, of contributing to it by complaining that I am the victim of attacks from Jewish leaders. But apart from the fact that I never categorize the sources of these attacks, it's extraordinary to accuse me of defending myself when I'm attacked. Why should I bend my back in the face of such abuse?

Official community bodies claim a dual mission: to combat anti-Semitism and to defend the Israeli government. However, the latter is taking precedence over the former. It's true that there's more to be done in this area. While anti-Semitism has not disappeared, it is very residual compared to past periods. It no longer stems from state institutions, but from individuals. And there are fewer and fewer of them. Anti-Semitic speech is a source of exclusion from political and media life. So much so that suspicion or accusation without proof is often enough. Conversely, Israel no longer exerts the fascination of the pioneering years or the "David versus Goliath" approach among the French population. Anti-Semitism is on the decline, but so is support for Israeli policy. From now on, institutions will evoke anti-Semitism above all to defend Israel.

The best proof is that they are very selective in their choice of allies. If they really believed, as they declare from every podium and/or column, that Jews are in danger in France, they would not sort out those who want to fight anti-Semitism. However, it has to be said that they refuse to help those who, at the same time, are critical of the Israeli government. On the contrary, they are roundly opposed.

Jewish organizations that are critical of the Israeli government are never highlighted, and are even opposed. Yet the Union des Juifs français pour la paix, Une autre voix juive and Trop c'est trop are all organizations that fight anti-Semitism. What's more, since it's accepted that the Middle East conflict is a source of anti-Semitism, without the official authorities complaining that French Jews are equated with Israelis, wouldn't it be a good way of combating anti-Semitism to highlight those Jews who offer a different image and who are proof of the diversity of the French Jewish community?

Once again, the dividing line is not between Jews and non-Jews, but between communitarians and universalists. It is unfortunate that, for so many reasons, many non-Jews have chosen to support the former and ignore, if not fight, the latter.

Conclusion, And... Enough!

I was the wrong person in the wrong place at the wrong time. Because a note that merely summarized a widely accepted situation should never have triggered such excessive reactions. A combination of circumstances led to the hysterization of the debate. At a time when the hope of peace was either near or inevitable—since the signing of the 1993 Oslo Accords—the resumption of the armed Intifada, the return of Ariel Sharon to power and his visit to the Temple Mount (the Esplanade of the Mosques in East Jerusalem) against the advice of the Israeli security forces, the Hamas attacks and the return to the cycle of repression/violence, peace seemed once again to be a distant horizon. Instead, the tendency was for each side to harden its tone and posture in order to negotiate from a position of strength. Support for Israel had largely waned in France. The myth of the small country fighting a mass of Arabs had long since disappeared in the face of Israel's military might.

The 1982 Lebanon war and the first Intifada, which began in 1987, had damaged Israel's moral credibility. The Oslo Accords put things back on track. But these were trampled underfoot. Despite the Hamas attacks—opposed by the Palestinian leadership—the return to power of Ariel Sharon, a long-standing opponent of the accords, and the resumption of repression eroded the French public's historic and "natural" support for the Israeli government in the conflict. This movement was all the more significant in left-wing opinion and at the base of the Socialist Party (PS), once an unwavering supporter of the Israeli cause. Worse still, my note had found its way to Lionel Jospin, who had given it a positive verdict. The risk was that the PS would distance itself from Israel under the impetus of its leader. My position was extremely modest, but I needed to set an example to dissuade anyone from following in my footsteps. The same note or article written by someone outside the PS would not have represented the same stakes.

A certain monopoly of communitarianism was called into question. Until now, only the Jewish community was supposed to have an influence on elections, and this led to a moderation of criticism of Israel, beyond anyone's assessment of the Israeli-Palestinian conflict, and even to the loudest possible expression of support for Tel Aviv, in order to attract a Jewish vote which officially does not exist, but which many people clearly want to seduce.

If the Arabs were also organized, they would carry more weight. I denounced this prospect when I was accused of provoking it, because it would only be a reflection of what was happening in the Jewish community. The fact is that attempts by French Arabs and/or Muslims to organize themselves have been fiercely opposed by the pro-Israeli lobby, which has put forward docile, pro-Israeli personalities. It's no coincidence that those with a falsified vision of secularism, forgetting the 1905 law's roots of freedom and tolerance, and very often zealous defenders of Israeli governments, are the first to describe any attempt at autonomous Arab organization as communitarian, while supporting Jewish community actions in the name of the fight against anti-Semitism. They demonize Muslim initiatives, most often with dubious amalgams and slanderous accusations.

The notorious weakening of support for the Israeli cause, both in France in general and on the left, had the almost systemic effect of radicalizing its supporters. Finally, by an unfortunate coincidence of timing, the attacks of September 11, 2001 occurred in this already heavy atmosphere, making the debate even more tense, as a few voices began to question the causes of terrorism. Ariel Sharon quickly took the opportunity to put an end to the debate, declaring: "We have our Bin Laden, and his name is Arafat." It was at this point that the pseudo-thesis "trying to understand terrorism is to legitimize it" began to flourish.

If I have expressed myself on these subjects, it is in the name of a certain idea of justice, a refusal of injustice and repression, strong convictions on the equality of human beings and peoples, the defense of freedoms and the right of peoples to self-determination, and to remain faithful to my ideals. In other words, exactly the same feelings that led me

Conclusion, And... Enough!

to be revolted by anti-Semitism and in favor of the existence of an Israeli state. I am opposed by people who believe that, for various reasons, Israel should not be considered as just any other state and that, in the end, it enjoys rights that would be denied to others. Or by people who think that since Jews have a lot of power, we should go along with them. Their anti-Semitic reasoning does not lead to hostility or hatred of Jews (although some use very harsh words in private), but to an alignment with what seems to be the will of the Jewish community.

People sometimes ask me if—knowing what was going to happen—I'd write the same note. I wouldn't change a single line, and if I have one regret, it's that my bad premonitions came true. It's not that I said them. Of course, I would have spared myself all the unpleasantness of this affair. I'd be more central in the public arena, and my books better documented and more widely distributed. IRIS would be much more important and my family would have been spared. IRIS did not disappear, and in fact continued to grow, thanks to the talent and energy of its team. But its growth would have been even greater. On the positive side, this has led us to innovate, to put more energy into our work. IRIS has gained in credibility, as a research center where speech is free and resists pressure from interest groups. I can continue to publish books, but many publishers have closed their doors to me. Nor have I disappeared from the media. But the weekly columns I enjoyed before this controversy, in *Nice-Matin* and *La Voix du Nord*, have ceased at the request of the regional CRIFs. And there are many media outlets, including *mainstream ones,* where I am blacklisted because of my positions. Conferences I attend are regularly cancelled at the request of those who demonize me. And many people prefer, when in doubt, not to take any risks.

I got into this business out of a spirit of freedom. The risks I've taken are minimal compared to those others have taken in more difficult times. The "courage" I'm recognized for regularly arouses spontaneous sympathy. Many people are grateful for the stands I take, and thank me for braving the prevailing winds. They praise my integrity, admitting that it is the cause of the attacks I suffer, and express their gratitude to me. The many testimonials to this effect are a source of comfort, and many people congratulate me on having stood my ground. I have neither given in to the sirens of anti-Semitism nor to those of the courtier spirit. They know that if I don't say everything I think, I mean everything I say, and that I don't make my analyses dependent on power struggles or possible "rewards". In this sense, I have remained faithful to the teenager of the Lycée Saint-Exupéry.

In addition to the family love that unites us, my wife and three sons also appreciate the dignity they feel I have shown in these difficult times. The look on their faces is worth all the unpleasantness.

Afterword: Letter from a Jewish Friend, by Fanny Weisselberger

Dear Pascal,

In 2001, shortly before we entered today's world, you wrote an article that was, unfortunately, to be remembered[72]. And not the best-intentioned ones. Sixteen years on, positions have scarcely changed and the situation seems to have stagnated. Persona non grata for some French Jews, but also for those guided by a "Jewish passion", the sword of Damocles is just waiting to pierce you. While stains on reputation are often fleeting, there is one that seems indelible. How can you avoid struggling with the old demon of anti-Semitism?

I had to wonder about the causes of such an accusation. Not believing it for a second in no way prevents reflection. Are you a victim of racial profiling? A victim of your outbursts? A victim of some of your "supporters"? Nothing of the sort,

---

72. Pascal Boniface, "Lettre à un ami israélien", *Le Monde,* August 3, 2001.

really. Victim of those whose narrow-mindedness seems to blind their thinking. Considering themselves attacked by your opinions, their response seems proportionate. Whether you're talking about geopolitics, soccer or even your passion for Léo Ferré, they hear Israel, Palestine, Jews, Arabs or even Shoah. When the Godwin point precedes the exchange, words give way to evils.

"I'd like to write my story so that others don't write it for me," you told me. If you lie down, it's only on paper. But it seems to me that there's more to it than that. You're appalled at the idea of still suffering the consequences of what you feel is a terrible injustice. Privately at first. Because you, the contact man, are whistled offside before the match has even started. And yet, those who know you know that nothing delights you more than an adversarial debate where ideas come face to face. Certainly for the love of democracy, but above all for the spirit of competition. But how can you debate with someone who has left the rational world to join the club of anti-Semitic extremists? Secondly, in public. After all, you have a baby of some thirty years and as many employees: the Institut de relations internationales et stratégiques (IRIS). You have had to learn to live with the fear of seeing it disappear overnight, in the face of those who *accuse*.

Although I've found you to be sometimes carried away, often relentless, I in no way consider you extreme. You would never tip over to the other side, quite simply because it's beyond your reach. This conviction, which I've built up by working directly alongside you, has never met with the slightest doubt. Otherwise, I couldn't have gone on another day. So, I'm here to re-establish my (the?) reality. The one I see when I talk to you, those who are *with* you, those who are *against* you, those who take the liberty of giving me their biased opinion when they don't simply explain to me that I should be wary of you. It's excessive talk, hearsay and accusations of intent that make me distrust you. It's differential treatment, unprincipled behaviour and lack of objectivity.

Finally, this book seems almost (too) late. We're past the stage of explanation, justification and understanding. We are now at the stage of *de-demonization*.

Appendix 1—The Middle East, socialists, international equity, electoral efficiency—Note by Pascal Boniface

Imagine: following a conflict, a country occupies territories in violation of international law. Thirty-four years later, this occupation continues despite the condemnations of the international community. The population living in these occupied territories is subjected to exorbitant constraints and exceptional laws, and denied the right to self-determination. Destruction of homes, confiscation of land, imprisonment without trial, daily humiliations and, until recently, torture legalized under the name of "moderate physical pressure" are commonplace. The population revolted, demanding the creation of an independent state on the occupied territories, which would simply be the application of the United Nations Charter. A cycle of violence and repression ensued, with the occupying power's security forces regularly shooting and killing demonstrators, and attacks claiming the lives of the occupying state's own population.

In any such situation, a humanist, let alone a man of the left, would condemn the occupying power.

Imagine a country where the Prime Minister has been directly involved in massacres of civilians, mainly women and children in unarmed refugee camps. A country where the leader of the third party in power calls members of one of the country's main national communities "snakes and even worse vipers" and proposes to "annihilate these villains, these bandits", to shoot them with supermissiles. A country where armed extremists can organize pogroms against unarmed civilians with impunity.

This would be an unacceptable situation. Yet it is accepted in the Middle East. How can we explain the fact that, in this particular case, the elementary principles of respect for others are systematically pilloried rather than violated?

Three elements are indisputable:

1° The Shoah was the most horrific treatment of the Jewish people. Although the word is increasingly overused, it is the only one to have suffered a real genocide, with the intention of totally exterminating them as a people. In the face of this trauma (the culmination of widespread anti-Semitic behavior), in which the Jewish people were very much alone, Israel represents sanctuary, the certainty that the worst will never happen again.

2° The democratic State of Israel (even if the Arab population does not have the same rights as the Jewish population) is surrounded by authoritarian, even dictatorial regimes, and has had to fight to have its existence recognized by its neighbors.

3° Israel's defense in these circumstances took precedence over everything else, including the principles that had inspired its creators.

These indisputable elements cannot justify the fact that the suffering of the Jewish people has given them the right to oppress others. To ensure that the Shoah never happens again, must we accept the violation of the rights of another people?

With reference to this trauma, all those who oppose the policies of the Israeli government are suspected of not condemning the Shoah or of being anti-Semitic.

But even if nothing has come to match the horror of the latter, this reasoning is now proving inadequate and even unacceptable.

It's true that there are anti-Semites among the pro-Palestinians. But they are in the minority, and cannot be used to suggest that those who call for universal principles to be applied in the Middle East are doing so out of hatred for the Jewish people.

- Today, the main victims are the Palestinians. You'd have to be insensitive to realities not to admit it. This is certainly not to say that they have done no wrong, that corruption does not exist there, that a historic opportunity was not lost by Arafat at Camp David, that there are no indiscriminate attacks, and so on. The fact remains, however, that the occupier and the occupied cannot be equated.

In any case, this is how most of the French population feels, especially young people. In this respect, I'm struck by the evolution of young people, especially students, who twenty years ago were very divided on the subject of the Middle East, but today are overwhelmingly pro-Palestinian.

- The link between the fight against anti-Semitism and the defense of Israel at all costs is short-sighted, and may even prove counter-productive. We won't fight anti-Semitism by legitimizing Israel's current repression of Palestinians. On the contrary, and unfortunately, it can be encouraged by doing so.

The intellectual terrorism of accusing those who do not accept the policies of Israeli governments (and not the State of Israel) of anti-Semitism pays off in the short term, but can prove catastrophic in the medium term. It does not diminish opposition to the Israeli government, but either modifies its expression, which may become more diffuse and insidious, or reinforces it and develops irritation towards the Jewish community. It isolates the Jewish community on a national level.

Fortunately, a few of its representatives, such as Rony Brauman and Pierre Vidal-Naquet, have publicly disassociated themselves from Israeli repression, preventing dreadful amalgams.

Creating a link between the fight against anti-Semitism and the support or non-condemnation of Sharon can hardly serve the first cause, far from it.

There are cases—we've seen similar ones in France—where a government's policy does a disservice to the nation it is supposed to serve. It is a disservice to that nation not to distance oneself from the government in question.

By betting on its electoral weight to allow the Israeli government to go unpunished, the Jewish community is also losing out in the medium term. The community of Arab and/or Muslim origin is also getting organized, it will want to act as a counterweight and, at least in France, will soon carry more weight if it hasn't already.

It would therefore be preferable for everyone to uphold universal principles, rather than the weight of each community.

By seeking to maintain an equal balance between Israeli forces of order and Palestinian demonstrators, by drawing a parallel between the attacks of desperate people who are ready to commit suicide because they have no other horizons, and the planned policy of repression implemented by the Israeli government, the SP and the government are seen by a growing proportion of public opinion as "unjust". Why does what applies to the Kosovars not apply to the Palestinians? Is it possible to *demonize* Haider and treat Sharon, who has not been content with verbal blunders but has taken action, as normal? These are remarks we hear more and more often. I'm struck by the number of young Beurs, French Muslims of all ages, who claim to be left-wing but who, referring to the situation in the Middle East, say they don't want to vote for Jospin in the presidential election.

An attitude judged to be unbalanced in the Middle East—and, of course, once again thought to be to the disadvantage of Arabs—confirms that the Arab-Muslim community is not taken into account or is even rejected by the Socialist family. The situation in the Middle East, and the Socialists' timidity in condemning Israeli repression, reinforces an identity-based withdrawal of Muslims in France that no one—Jew, Muslim, Christian or pagan—can welcome.

It's better to lose an election than your soul. But by equating the Israeli government with the Palestinians, we simply risk losing both. Is support for Sharon worth losing 2002?

It's high time the French Socialist Party abandoned a position which, while intended to be balanced between the Israeli government and the Palestinians, is becoming increasingly abnormal due to the reality of the situation on the ground, and is increasingly perceived as such, and which, moreover, does not serve—but on the contrary serves—the medium/long-term interests of the Israeli people, and of the French Jewish community.

Appendix 2

RÉPUBLIQUE FRANÇAISE

MINISTÈRE DE L'INTÉRIEUR ,

DE LA SÉCURITE INTÉRIEURE ET DES LIBERTÉS LOCALES

LE MINISTRE

CAB.INT/BDC/n°4541/CJ

Paris, le 1 DEC. 2002

Monsieur le Directeur,

La campagne suscitée par l'interview que vous avez accordée au journal suisse *Le Temps* est parvenue jusqu'à moi.

À tous mes interlocuteurs, j'ai répondu qu'il ne m'appartenait pas de prendre position **quant aux propos tenus par un intellectuel dans l'exercice de ses fonctions.**

J'ai néanmoins pris connaissance avec attention de l'eclairage que vous avez bien voulu m'apporter et vous prie de croire, Monsieur le Directeur, en l'assurance de mes sentiments les meilleurs.

Nicolas SARKOZY

Monsieur Pascal BONIFACE

Directeur de l'institut de relations internationales et stratégiques, 2 bis, rue Mercœur

75011 PARIS

Appendix 3

Parti Socialiste

Secrétariat National
Aux relations internationales

10, rue de Solférino
75333 Paris Cedex 07
Tél. : 01 45 56 77 00
Fax : 01 47 05 15 78
www.parti-socialiste.fr

Nos Réf. PM/ncm N°03.015

Paris, le 8 septembre 2003

Monsieur Ménotti BOTTAZZI
55 rue du vieil Armand
68540 BOLLWILLER

Cher Camarade,

Je réponds à ta lettre du 27 août, dont j'apprécie la sincérité. Elle mériterait, bien sûr, de plus amples développements, mais je me contenterai de deux remarques :

1. **Non, Pascal BONIFACE n'a pas été « débarqué », ni « licencié » de ses responsabilités pour délit d'opinion.** Je connais Pascal depuis longtemps, nous avons beaucoup travaillé ensemble professionnellement, je reconnais sa compétence et son talent, et je souhaite qu'il continue à être utile à nos idées. Si je ne partage pas tout à fait ton jugement sur son livre – qui comporte à la fois, selon moi, des analyses justes et d'autres plus contestables – je défends absolument son droit à défendre ses opinions. Celles-ci ont, par leur force, provoqué un débat, suscité des polémiques. La direction du Parti socialiste a estimé, après le Congrès de Dijon, qu'il était mieux, pour notre parti comme pour Pascal BONIFACE que la responsabilité qu'il occupait ne pâtisse pas de cette confrontation et de ses excès, et qu'il s'en retire pour un temps, d'autant qu'il ne l'occupait plus guère depuis la fameuse « note » de 2001.
Je m'en suis expliqué avec lui, longuement et amicalement. D'autres prises de positions ont entraîné un retrait plus marqué de sa part ; je le regrette, et ferai tout pour qu'il ne soit que provisoire.

2. **S'agissant du fond, je partage beaucoup de tes constats.** Face au drame du Proche-Orient, les Socialistes ne doivent servir qu'une seule cause, celle de la paix entre des Israéliens – je te cite – « vivant dans des frontières sûres et reconnues» et des Palestiniens ayant un « État viable ». Cette position d'équilibre est exigeante, elle suppose de mettre chacun devant ses responsabilités. Ainsi le Parti socialiste condamne-t-il les attentats terroristes aussi bien que les ripostes ciblées, et regrette-t-il l'édification du « mur de séparation ». Défendre ces exigences est et sera notre ligne de conduite (je t'adresse, pour en témoigner, le texte publié sous ma signature concernant la « feuille de route », malheureusement en grande difficulté). Crois que j'y veillerai.

Je crois en revanche inexact, et même complètement faux, de prétendre que la position du Parti socialiste serait unilatéralement « pro-israélienne » - pas davantage qu'elle n'est « pro-palestinienne » et qu'il serait interdit d'y « critiquer Israël » ! Les soupçons de communautarisme ou de complaisance sont, nous concernant, totalement déplacés. La critique de chacun des acteurs est pour nous, non seulement un droit, mais un devoir. Exerçons-la à l'égard de tous les protagonistes de cette terrible affaire.

Je te prie de croire, Cher Camarade, en mes sentiments les meilleurs.

Pierre MOSCOVICI
Secrétaire National
Aux Relations Internationales

The Anti-Semite

Appendix 4

>Manuel Valls
Maire d'Evry - Député de l'Essonne

Cher Pascal,

Merci pour ton mot suite à mon papier dans
le Monde. Je suis de tout cœur avec toi à [illegible] de tes
analyses sur le Proche-Orient. [illegible]

adresse:
Mairie - place des droits
de l'homme et du citoyen
91011 Evry cedex

tél:
01 60 91 60 92

fax:
01 60 77 17 95

mel:
maire@mairie-evry.fr

Table of contents

From the same author

at Max Milo

Je t'aimais bien, tu sais. Le monde et la France : le désamour ?, 2017.
Les pompiers pyromanes, 2015.

with other publishers

La géopolitique [5th ed.], Eyrolles, 2018.
50 idées reçues sur l'état du monde [8th ed.], Armand Colin, 2018.
Comprendre le monde [4th ed.], Armand Colin, 2017.
Les relations internationales de 1945 à nos jours, Eyrolles, 2017.
Géopolitique du sport, Armand Colin, 2016.
Léo Ferré, toujours vivant, La Découverte, 2016.

Atlas du monde global (co-written with Hubert Védrine) [3rd ed.], Armand Colin, 2015.
Atlas des crises et des conflits (co-written with Hubert Védrine) [3rd ed.], Armand Colin, 2016.

Best sellers Max Milo Editions

Hitler's banker, Jean-François Bouchard

Confessions of a forger, Éric Piedoie Le Tiec

The Koran and the flesh, Ludovic-Mohamed Zahed

Governing by fake news, Jacques Baud

Governing by chaos, Collectif

A political history of food, Paul Ariès

Mad in U.S.A.: The ravages of the "American model",
Michel Desmurget

Mondial soccer club geopolitics, Kévin Veyssière

Putin: Game master?, Jacques Braud

Treatise on the three impostors: Moses, Jesus, Muhammad,
The Spirit of Spinoza

TV Lobotomy, Michel Desmurget